THE LIVING ROOM SERIES

ALL THINGS NEW

A STUDY ON
2 CORINTHIANS

KELLY MINTER

LifeWay Press® Nashville, Tennessee

Published by LifeWay Press® • ©2016 Kelly Minter • Reprint November 2016

ISBN 9781430055044
Item 006103969
Dewey decimal classification: 227.3
Subject heading: BIBLE. N.T. 2 CORINTHIANS—STUDY AND TEACHING / CHRISTIAN LIFE / REGENERATION

To order additional copies of this resource, write LifeWay Church Resources Customer Service; One LifeWay Plaza; Nashville, TN 37234-0113; FAX order to 615.251.5933; call toll-free 800.458.2772; email *orderentry@lifeway.com;* order online at *www.lifeway.com;* or visit the LifeWay Christian Store serving you.

Printed in the United States of America

Adult Ministry Publishing, LifeWay Church Resources, One LifeWay Plaza, Nashville, TN 37234-0152

Author's literary agent is D.C. Jacobson & Associates LLC, an Author Management Company, *www.dcjacobson.com.*

TABLE OF CONTENTS

Join Kelly at

 cultivate

A Women's Gathering Around the Word

AT A CULTIVATE EVENT, YOU'LL EXPERIENCE:

BIBLICAL TEACHING

ACOUSTIC WORSHIP

PRAYER

A HEART FOR MISSIONS

Dates and locations available at
cultivatevent.com

MEET THE AUTHOR
KELLY MINTER

KELLY MINTER IS AN AUTHOR, SPEAKER, AND SONGWRITER. SHE IS PASSIONATE ABOUT WOMEN DISCOVERING JESUS THROUGH THE PAGES OF SCRIPTURE. SO WHETHER IT'S THROUGH STUDY, SONG, OR THE SPOKEN WORD, KELLY'S DESIRE IS TO AUTHENTICALLY EXPRESS CHRIST TO THE WOMEN OF THIS GENERATION. SHE HAS FOUND DEEP HOPE AND HEALING THROUGH THE BIBLE'S TRUTHS, MAKING HER MESSAGE PERSONAL AND RELATIONAL.

No Other Gods, the first installment of The Living Room Series, helps women unveil the false gods in their lives for the ultimate purpose of discovering freedom in the one, true God. *Ruth: Loss, Love & Legacy* follows the redemptive story of Ruth, displaying God's providence and purpose even in the most trying circumstances. *Nehemiah: A Heart That Can Break* is an unforgettable journey into the missional heart of God. *What Love Is: The Letters of 1, 2, 3 John* look at the words of the Beloved Disciple regarding life in Christ. All studies are presented in the same Living Room Series format (studies can be done in any order). Kelly also released her first memoir, *Wherever The River Runs: How A Forgotten People Renewed My Hope In The Gospel,* about her life-changing journeys to the Amazon jungle.

Kelly writes extensively and speaks at women's conferences and events around the country. She has her own event called Cultivate: A Women's Gathering Around The Word. This Biblically based and stylistically simple event is for women of all ages. Kelly also partners closely with Justice and Mercy International, an organization that cares for the vulnerable and forgotten in the Amazon and Moldova. Kelly's music includes *Loss, Love, & Legacy,* which complements her Ruth study and most recently the worshipful *Hymns & Hallelujahs* which features songs from the *All Things New* video sessions. To view more about Kelly's studies, books, music, and calendar, visit *www.kellyminter.com.*

ALL THINGS NEW

INTRODUCTION

If you had asked me at the top of writing this study why I wanted to spend a year in 2 Corinthians, I would have pointed to all those wonderful passages like the thorn in the flesh, Christ's power in our weakness, the heavenly bodies we will one day receive, God's comfort in suffering, and a whole two chapters on generosity. These passages have been like firm trellises throughout my life, around which I've wrapped myself as the winds blew or the rains came or even when the warm sun shined. I've literally grown up on these beloved texts.

One of the earliest spiritual metaphors I learned was from 2 Corinthians, where Paul talks about carrying the treasures of knowing Jesus in fragile jars of clay. This has been especially meaningful to me because I've always longed to be a more steadfast, high-performing Christian. However, my best and truest efforts have never amounted to what I needed them to—at my core I have always been dyed-in-the-wool earthen. I simply cannot get away from this. But after meditating on Paul's words I'm reminded I don't have to. "For when I am weak, then I am strong" (2 Cor. 12:10). The page where this verse resides is well worn in every Bible I've ever owned.

Perhaps more than anything it is this weakness and honesty with which Paul writes that has so moved me. Scholars have often described 2 Corinthians as Paul's most personal letter, and this may be one of the reasons I never tire of returning to its pages. For the sufferer, Paul writes to us about the Father of unrivaled comfort and compassion. It is a passionate, pleading, even provocative letter at times, where Paul lays bare his outstretched heart to a community of somewhat inconsistent believers who frankly don't seem to care for him as much as he does them. Paul's heartbreak over their failures and enthusiasm over their restoration remind us of how relational the ministry of the gospel is. I just don't ever want to forget that if I lose my heart for people I've lost the purpose of ministry.

Speaking of ministry, if your only experience with the Christian faith has been rule-bound and oppressive, well then, might I invite you to the new covenant version? Paul spends valuable ink explaining that, since the coming of Christ, the ministry of the gospel is more gracious, humble, powerful, Spirit-filled, life-giving, and freeing than we ever imagined. He seems to sum the whole thing up in one word: glorious.

So that is how I began—eager to write about all the things I knew I loved about 2 Corinthians. Yet, after having immersed myself in the text, I discovered it was the passages less familiar to me that have so surprised and changed me. My hope is that you too might discover afresh a letter you thought you already knew. And if you've never done a Bible study before, all the more reason for you to explore its pages. One of the great anchors of Paul's letter is that Christianity isn't for the religious elite—I promise, the Corinthians will do a great job of backing this up. I warmly invite you, seasoned believer or new explorer, on a journey through this ancient letter.

The old has passed away; behold the new has come.

ALL THINGS NEW

GROUP DISCUSSION:

What do you hope to gain from this study and the time spent together?

Kelly says the gospel is made for real life and that the church of God is meant to thrive in real life. What does that mean to you?

Why do we have such an aversion to admitting weakness? What is Paul's overall message about weakness?

When a relationship becomes painful do you tend to close your heart to protect yourself or keep it open? What was Paul's response to the Corinthians who misunderstood him? How can we learn from him?

When you hear the statement, "Jesus came to make all things new," how do you respond? Why is there such hope in that statement?

From this introduction to 2 Corinthians, what do you most look forward to diving into? Explain.

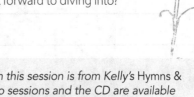

The music featured in this session is from Kelly's Hymns & Hallelujahs *CD. Video sessions and the CD are available for purchase at* LIFEWAY.COM/ALLTHINGSNEW

THE CHURCH IN A CITY

My friend Kelly is a twentysomething singer/songwriter. She's growing up in the thick of country music land, navigating the weeds of fame while plucking the daisies of getting to be artistic for a living. I'd asked Kelly to be part of a group that would work through the personal study and provide feedback. She obliged and offered great insight. You wouldn't believe how refining the process is for a manuscript when a group of women of all ages and demographics take their minds and the Holy Spirit inside them to the Word. Kelly, Amy, Jessica, Marcie, Julie, Julee, Karen, and Karen (lots of same names) brought their wisdom and sometimes their pushback to the table. What you hold in your hands is all the better for it.

At the culmination of our study, Kelly asked if we could meet for coffee, even though she doesn't drink coffee, poor soul. She had some things she wanted to discuss regarding 2 Corinthians. We jotted a date on the calendar because you don't have to ask me twice to meet you for coffee, conversation, and Corinthians. That's almost too much goodness for one morning! We slid two chairs up to the reclaimed wood bar, because everything in this world is now made of reclaimed wood. (I don't know if you've noticed this. I suppose all this wood in its original state was just claimed wood—people saw a log and claimed it. Now it's reclaimed. In 100 years will everything be reclaimed reclaimed wood? I wonder about these things.)

In some ways, Kelly's mulling over 2 Corinthians yielded more revelation than questions. She'd become acquainted with the problems in Corinth—its lust for power, zeal for social status, penchant for pleasure, vulnerability to deception so similar to our own—and noticed Paul's message was not only different from the prevailing mantras of the day, but that he actually swam against the current, dodging the culture and all its values that were rushing past him downstream. Paul was headed to a different destination. He was on mission for Jesus. And when your mission is different than what the world pines after, you'll find yourself maneuvering through the oncoming crowds.

"Everything is the opposite!" Kelly said, lifting her tea in the air. "I mean everything Paul says is like the exact opposite of what we're told we're supposed to live for." (Toss in the flash and fame of the music industry, and the opposites become polar.)

I knew what Kelly meant. After nearly a year in this letter, I too felt the inescapable tension between Paul's life and the life of ease and comfort. But Paul champions the paradoxical life of a believer with

unfathomable love. Here are just a few of the opposites: Our celebrity industry prizes youth, beauty, and, in many ways, perfection, while Paul writes about boasting in our weaknesses so Christ can receive the glory. We're taught to be razor-sharp competent so we can claw our way to the top of our businesses, but Paul says our competency exists so we can be better ministers. When someone offends us, we batten down the doors and windows of our hearts so as not to be invaded again. However, to a church who'd bruised Paul, he returned with both hands on either side of his heart stretching it as wide as it would reach. When we finally get a little authority handed to us we think it's for bossing everyone around, but could it be our authority is for building people up and working for their joy? Paul thought so. Our instincts tell us to hang onto our money so we can spend it on ourselves and have plenty for later, while Paul points to a poor church in Macedonia who wanted to give what little money it had away because the members saw it not as a duty but—get this—a privilege.

Paul champions the paradoxical life of a believer with unfathomable love.

No doubt Kelly was onto something. The Christian life is indeed one of paradox. What Jesus holds dear is opposite of what we in our natural states cling to. What struck me about our conversation, though, was that Kelly's acute revelation hadn't left her deflated or guilt-ridden. She didn't come saddened by the text. On the contrary, she was relieved. She found Paul's message remarkably freeing.

She was happy to know she can still love music and write songs and flutter from stage to stage like the cutest warbling morning bird, but she no longer has to do it for the fluctuating approval of humans. Of course, this will be a struggle, but she knows anew that in everything she puts her hand to she can—she must—concern herself with whether she's pleasing Jesus. She need not concern herself with keeping in step with the latest fads when being commended by Him is the highest praise. He is the One that satisfies. And it won't matter if her career lands her on the grandest stage in NYC or in the choir pew of a country church; however the Lord wants to use her gift will be her joy. And whomever the Lord brings across her path will be her ministry.

Yep, 2 Corinthians is a letter of opposites. A letter about discovering the quiet joys of swimming upstream, despite the hoots and hollers from quick pleasures that zip by us with the current. It's a letter about the adventurous faith of hanging all our hope on God, even though trusting our strength and pride to get us by almost always seems safer and more familiar. It's about an abiding peace at the ocean floor of our souls that oddly doesn't roll in after a visit to the spa, more assets in the portfolio, or a new white kitchen. Instead of having to earn or buy our peace, peace comes when our sins are no longer counted against us because God sent His Son Jesus into the world, who took our sins upon Himself. Paul calls this reconciliation.

As you work your way through 2 Corinthians, be on the lookout for opposites. Note the way Paul unconditionally loves the Corinthians, what he rejoices in, whom he trusts, and what he calls home. Do this, then think about what the world loves, what it celebrates, hopes in, and lays its head upon in the wee hours of the night. As you consider the striking differences, never forget you've been empowered to live beautifully and blatantly set apart because—since Jesus' death and resurrection—the old has gone, the new has come. And last time I checked, old and new are as opposite as they come.

DAY 1
A SEEMINGLY UNLIKELY PLACE FOR A CHURCH

2 CORINTHIANS 1:1-2

CORINTHIAN CHRONOLOGY:

A.D. 50-51
Paul establishes church in Corinth

A.D. 52
Writes instructive letter. (1 Cor. 5:9) This letter is lost.

A.D. 53-54
Writes 1 Corinthians.

A.D. 54
Makes "sorrowful visit" to Corinth.

A.D. 54
Writes "painful letter" (2 Cor. 2:3-4). This letter is lost.

A.D. 54
Writes 2 Corinthians

A.D. 56
Makes final visit to Corinth1

Whenever I visit a city I've never been to before, I start Googling it to death. Something about seeing the actual landscape of a place, eating at its restaurants, and strolling its well-known streets make me want to better understand its history and happenings. And, of course, determine what movie stars live there. The same is true when I start studying a book of the Bible. Learning about context and historical placement is vital to gaining a more accurate understanding of the book at hand.

Before we begin reading 2 Corinthians, let's set the stage with a few important elements we'll refer to throughout the study. Reconstructing the time line of Paul's visits and letters to the Corinthians is not without complications, but doing so gives us a good handle on the setting. Paul first visited Corinth and established the church there in A.D. 50-51. We learn from 1 Corinthians 5:9 that he wrote an instructive letter that is now lost. After hearing about significant problems in the church, Paul wrote the letter we know as 1 Corinthians around A.D. 53-54. Closely following that letter, he wrote what is referred to as the "sorrowful letter," also presumed to be lost. This brings us to 2 Corinthians, which Paul wrote in response to hearing the church had a few victories along with several failures that needed to be addressed. We'll become well acquainted with these issues in the days ahead, issues that will feel surprisingly familiar to us 2,000 years later.

LET'S BEGIN THIS JOURNEY TOGETHER BY LOOKING AT THE FIRST TWO VERSES OF 2 CORINTHIANS. READ 2 CORINTHIANS 1:1-2.

Paul was writing to the church of God at _____

Think of the most culturally electrifying city you've ever visited. You may have memories awash with the arts and sporting events, a shopping spree surrounded by bustling commerce. You may have taken in a play or a movie, or had your senses stirred with ancient paintings or relics while strolling through museums. Perhaps you grabbed a hot dog from a steaming street cart or followed a waiter in a tuxedo to the finest meal your fork has ever pierced—a great city has both frankfurter and filet. You certainly spotted the wealthy being chauffeured about town, possibly at the same time you heard coins tumbling into the cup of the homeless. If you're like my sister, Katie, you spotted a celebrity—she finds them everywhere she goes. (She attributes this to putting on her "famous eyes" as soon as she gets to a popular destination.) Bright lights and garish signs, taxi horns and symphonies, violence and class, rich and poor, and everyone in between, trying to find their way in this place we've known since nearly the beginning of time: the city.

You could make the argument that first-century Corinth was the citiest of cities.

The ancient city of Corinth boasted everything you could ever want. But as we know: having access to everything we could ever want doesn't always end up being what we thought we wanted.

When Paul arrived in the early A.D. 50s, Corinth was at the pinnacle of its development. A commercial epicenter of southern Greece, perched on an isthmus (think Seattle) that brimmed with tourists and trade due to its two harbors, Lechaeum and Cenchreae, Corinth was thriving, wealthy, and steeped in a blend of Roman and Greek culture. Tourists and locals could indulge in every good imaginable from wines to linens, olive oil to fresh drinking water, spices and meats, while inhaling the sea breeze rolling in through the ports where merchants and travelers came and went. A destination for world-class sporting events and entertainment drew the masses to this metropolis of approximately 80,000 people with 20,000 more on the outskirts. The ancient city of Corinth boasted everything you could ever want. But as we know: having access to everything we could ever want doesn't always end up being what we thought we wanted.

The richness of Corinth's culture had its downside, as do our own modern day cities. Prostitution, slavery, foreign pagan practices, poverty, and sexual perversion of all kinds coalesced within its territory. The term *Corinthianize* as even coined to describe debauchery and moral baseness that certainly didn't originate in Corinth, but was celebrated there. False gods were everywhere. The temple of Aphrodite, the Greek goddess of love and life, was a central shrine in Corinth. As one put it, Corinth was the "Vanity Fair" of Rome.[2]

PERSONAL TAKE: *Given this information, describe what could be surprising about Paul writing to the church in Corinth.*

TURN TO ACTS 18:1-11 AND READ ABOUT PAUL'S FIRST VISIT TO CORINTH. WE'LL GATHER SOME BASIC FACTS FROM THIS PASSAGE, SO THINK FROM THE PERSPECTIVE OF A REPORTER.

What couple did Paul live with and what country had they moved from?

What type of work did Paul do to support himself?
❑ *cut hair*   ❑ *make tents*
❑ *fish*   ❑ *all of the above*

What two people groups did he teach in the synagogues?
Jews and _____ .

According to verse 8, what happened to many of the Corinthians Paul taught?

How long did Paul stay and teach God's Word to the Corinthians?
❑ *1 ½ Years*   ❑ *2 years*
❑ *6 months*   ❑ *12 years*

Looking back at the second paragraph of today's lesson, when did Paul first arrive in Corinth? Early A.D. _____ .

Your Bible may show in red the Lord's direct words to Paul in Acts 18:9-10. Where did the Lord tell Paul He had many people?

One night the Lord spoke to Paul in a vision: "Do not be afraid; keep on speaking, do not be silent. For I am with you, and no one is going to attack and harm you, because I have many people in this city."
Acts 18:9-10, HCSB

This is a comforting and encouraging word for wherever we live.

PERSONAL REFLECTION: *You may not live in the heart of a major city, but most of us live well within the reach of a city's influence. In the columns below, describe the benefits and obstacles of being a believer in Jesus in a wildly diverse place like "the city."*

BENEFITS	OBSTACLES

One of the reasons I'm passionate about 2 Corinthians is because of how relative it feels at this time in my life and in the culture in which I live. If the church worked in Corinth, it can work in the places you and I inhabit. I admit that sometimes I think our world is too far gone with abuse, racism, and moral depravation. However, if the gospel of Jesus transformed Corinth's prostitutes, arrogantly religious, oppressively wealthy, pagans, farmers, merchants, athletes, slaves, and synagogue leaders (like the one you just read about in Acts 18), then the good news of Jesus Christ can transform the people of our cities today. And though I'm tempted at times to think that God's people are only found in religious settings, God had His people in Corinth. In the city. Just like He has you and me in the cultural settings we live in.

READ THE OPENING LINES OF 1 CORINTHIANS 1:2 BELOW:

To the church of God in Corinth, to those sanctified in Christ Jesus and called to be his holy people, together with all those everywhere who call on the name of our Lord Jesus Christ—their Lord and ours:

Paul gives an additional description of the believers in Corinth: To those _____ in Christ Jesus.

Hagiazo: to make holy, i.e. (ceremonially) purify or consecrate ... hallow, be holy, sanctify.[4] When God saves us we're purified and set apart for His purposes.

If Paul were writing to a group of monks or nuns you might think, *Okay, they've got a good shot at this holiness, sanctification, purity thing.* But to people in the middle of a wide-open boomtown like Corinth, with no prior history of Christianity, to be seen in God's eyes as holy?[3] (See margin for definition.) Second Corinthians reminds us that God's church shines most brightly in the darkness rather than in already-lit sanctuaries.

PERSONAL REFLECTION: *What specifically about your culture makes it difficult for you to live a holy life? (Don't even think about writing down a generic answer on our first day together. Write what's hard for you in your culture. Be specific.)*

In the days ahead we'll see Paul pursuing God's people with unrivaled fervor. They were a struggling church that had bought into the trends and passions of the environment in which they lived. As one writer put it, "Many of their faults can be traced to their uncritical acceptance of the attitudes, values, and behaviors of the society in which they lived."[5] Uncritical acceptance. I can relate to this. If I'm not alert and aware, I can uncritically accept the prominent whims of the day and hardly realize it.

PERSONAL REFLECTION: *Without a judgmental spirit, how have you seen the Western church at large uncritically accept certain cultural norms that are blatantly unbiblical?*

We'll dig much deeper into Scripture in the coming days, but today I wanted you to understand the context of what we'll be studying. I'm excited to journey with you as we examine together what some have called Paul's most personal letter.

Dear friend, as you embark on this study, know you are not alone. As Paul put it best in his opening words, we're in this together, *with all the saints.*

> **PERSONAL RESPONSE:** *I have no doubt the Lord is going to surprise you over the next eight weeks. What is your single greatest hope in studying 2 Corinthians?*

DAY 2
THE GOD OF
ALL COMFORT

2 CORINTHIANS 1:3-11

I once held the idea that if I followed the principles laid out for me in Scripture, if I loved God and made solid, biblical choices, I would be blessed with some version of a really good life, void of heartbreak or catastrophe or sickness. As I grew older, I gradually realized that following God didn't guarantee this premium package, this safeness. I'd seen really godly people suffer and read about such believers in Scripture. Still, I somehow felt that if I did my part then God would be obligated to do His: build me the kind of life we covet here in America and protect me from pain. This seemed like such a reasonable expectation.

> For in bringing many sons to glory, it was entirely appropriate that God —all things exist for Him and through Him—should make the source of their salvation perfect through sufferings.
> Hebrews 2:10, HCSB

For the record, I do believe obedience yields blessing and that God delights in giving us material and relational gifts, often in response to our following Him. Even still, my understanding of how suffering fit—or didn't fit—into the bigger paradigm of the Christian faith was deficient. The Bible reveals that suffering has its place in our lives, even Hebrews 2:10 explains that Jesus was made perfect through suffering. What I'd missed all those years of pining for what made me feel good and attempting to protect myself from whatever I feared "coming upon me" (in the words of Job) was really quite simple: suffering is part of the blessing.

I hope this brings more relief to you than alarm. The thought of suffering shouldn't thrust a bolt of terror through our hearts because as we will study today, God is especially present in our suffering. But neither should we set out for a life of pain, martyrdom, and victimhood in Jesus' name. We've been around the woe-is-me people in their Gap® sackcloth, and they're painfully not enjoyable. Bottom line, we shouldn't fear suffering, but we don't need to be looking under rocks for it either.

READ 2 CORINTHIANS 1:3-11.

In verse 3 Paul praises God as the Father of _____ and the God of all _____.

List every positive you can find about suffering in these verses. Take your time, considering even indirect benefits.

You've already noted that Paul opens his letter to the Corinthians by acknowledging two of God's characteristics that meet us in our afflictions (trouble or tribulations). Notice the impact of Paul's phrase in verse 3, "Father of mercies" (or compassion). Paul didn't say that God is a merciful Father, though He is, rather that He's the Father of mercies. He's the very source and origin of all compassion. He is compassion's first and only fountain— the Father from whom all compassion flows. This is a paradigm shift for the person who sees God as someone who only occasionally taps into His kind side.

Let's consider the original language of the word *mercies* (compassion). The Greek word is *oiktirmos* and is used only five times in the New Testament. It means "Bowels in which compassion resides, a heart of compassion, emotions, longings, manifestations of pity"[6] or "the inward parts."[7] When we look at the definition of this word, we get a strong sense of feeling. According to Scripture, I want you to hear today that the Lord feels for you.

LOOK UP PHILIPPIANS 3:10.

Paul's goal was to know the power of Christ's resurrection but he also wanted to share in His sufferings. What benefit came with this? (A specific word is used.)

TURN BACK AND READ 2 CORINTHIANS 1:5.

In this passage Paul states that Christ's sufferings overflow into our lives. What do you think this means?

When Paul talks about the sufferings of Christ spilling over into our lives, he could mean a few overlapping ideas: 1. Sufferings on account of Christ. 2. Sufferings ordained for us by Christ. 3. Sufferings associated with Christ. 4. Sufferings like Christ endured. What I believe is important for us to know is that as believers, we will suffer certain things that are distinct to our association with Christ. Many Christians are suffering severe persecution around the world while others are hurting in lesser, but still painful, ways for their faith. For example, you may have been passed over for a promotion, lost a job, endured ridicule from friends, been betrayed or abandoned, all because of your belief in Jesus. Paul realized there is a certain fellowship that takes place with Jesus in times of suffering because no one knows suffering better than He does. It's part of His territory.

PERSONAL REFLECTION: *How have you become more deeply acquainted with Jesus as a result of sharing with Him in His sufferings?*

I've yet to meet a person who enjoys suffering, but I've met many who've found intimacy with Jesus in the midst of their suffering. There are certain parts of Jesus you just can't know on a path of ease, and once you've tasted that closeness with Him you wouldn't trade it for the smooth course. In addition to experiencing a special fellowship with Jesus (Phil. 3:10), Paul reveals another reason why suffering brings blessing.

Whenever Christ's sufferings overflow into our lives what overflows out of us (2 Cor. 1:5)? This is so awesome to me!

In the city of Manaus, Brazil, there's a natural phenomenon called *The Meeting of the Waters.* This is where the Rio Negro and Rio Solimoes meet and form what the Brazilians determine to be the official start of the Amazon River. The Rio Negro is black and looks like a river of Coke®; The Rio Solimoes appears to be flowing with coffee and cream. (These are my best scientific descriptions.) When you sail on this part of the Amazon, you're floating down one grand body of water that's made up of two rivers distinct in appearance, temperature, minerals, and speed. Even though the Negro and Solimoes don't appear to mix for several miles, they are one. And as Christ's sufferings and comfort can also seem incongruent, you will never have one without the other—the sufferings of Christ and His comfort flow together. As Charles H. Spurgeon put it, "when the scale of trials is full, you will find the scale of consolation just as heavy."[8]

PERSONAL REFLECTION: *As you look back on what you have suffered, how has Christ's comfort met you at every turn? As you consider your response, know that our pain can often cloud our ability to see the goodness of God. So depend on the truth of Scripture.*

Look back at 2 Corinthians 1:8-9. Though we don't know the specific trials Paul endured:
1. Where did they take place?

2. What effect did they have on Paul?

What reason does Paul give in verse 9 for having gone through these hardships?

PERSONAL RESPONSE: *When has your pain caused you to rely on God instead of yourself (you may be in the midst of this right now)? How has the transfer from depending on yourself to God changed you? What have you learned about your own limitations and about God's inexhaustible, resurrection power? Take some time with this. And if you're not experiencing Him in your suffering, ask Him to help you identify His comfort in your trial.*

According to verse 10, where does all of Paul's hope lie?

One of the most beautiful declarations in all of Scripture is found in verse 4, "He comforts us in all our afflictions, so that we may be able to comfort those who are in any kind of affliction" (HCSB). When we traverse through difficulty, it's often hard to see outside of our pain. But we find great purpose in our suffering when we realize our experiences will serve as unique comforts to others going through similar trials.

Describe a season when someone brought you timely comfort because God had ministered to him or her in a trial similar to your own?

If we want to be able to comfort others with the comfort we've received from God, we need to be "comfort-able." What I mean is that I've experienced times in my life where I didn't want to be comforted or didn't know how to be, where I was plain mad and determined to sulk under anger's roof. If we find ourselves in a situation where we are inconsolable, unable to be comforted or encouraged, there is a problem. Receiving comfort requires humility and vulnerability before the Lord, open hands that say we don't know it all or have it all and need our Savior.

After working through this study, a friend of mine shared that the phrase, "On him we have set our hope" (2 Cor. 1:10) had at one time been a lifeline for her. She was pregnant with a child whom the doctors were concerned would not survive. In the midst of her pregnancy, she said she "envisioned hanging all my hope on the Lord as if on a hook." She couldn't hang her hope on her husband, her other children, the doctors, not even on her precious child surviving. She could only hang her whole life's hope singularly on the Lord, regardless of what might come. She tenderly shared with our group that her child did not linger long on this earth but her hope in the Lord remains.

God's comfort is overflowing in nature.

As the Negro and Solimoes rivers flow as one, Christ's suffering and His comfort run together in our lives, side-by-side. As Christians, we never have to suffer without Christ's comfort, and I believe there are certain comforts we will never know apart from His suffering. If you are plodding through a trial, perhaps an unbearable one far beyond your ability to endure, draw from God's comfort that runs straight through the person of Jesus into your life. He promises it in measure to your pain. And when you're met with God's consolation, you'll be eager to bind up the wounds of another person who's in similar pain because God's comfort is overflowing in nature. You'll have more than enough to share.

DAY 3
A CHANGE OF PLANS

2 CORINTHIANS 1:12-24

The strangest thing is happening to me. Suddenly parent-isms have been tumbling into my vocabulary. You don't need to be a parent for this to happen; you simply have to have had parents. For instance, when the milk is a week past its expiration date I now say, "It's perfectly fine," which my mom used to say about anything that had the current year stamped on the carton. I am also a huge employer of one of my dad's favorite expressions, "Good grief." My friends distance themselves whenever I use it in public—which is all the time. Growing up, one of my mom's most common phrases in response to my badgering her about something I wanted to do was, "We'll see." It took me 20 years to realize this was code for, "The answer is 9 percent no way, kiddo," but hope springs eternal. I use "we'll see," all the time with my nieces and nephews. It's a great way to hedge your bets, especially if you might need to change your plans.

As we go along, we'll discover that Paul was anything but a "we'll see" kind of guy. His yes was yes and his no was no, but this didn't mean he never had to change his plans. In today's reading, Paul will explain to the Corinthians why he didn't visit them when he originally intended. We'll also discover a few things about how the Corinthians felt about this.

READ 2 CORINTHIANS 1:12-24.

If there's one thing about studying 2 Corinthians that's challenged me personally, it's that Paul doesn't shy away from difficult relationships. We'll get into this further, but the Corinthians had some issues with Paul, and his not showing up when he said he would was one of them. But before Paul jumps into an explanation of his actions, he first establishes his heart toward them.

Revisit verse 12. Paul and his friends have related to the Corinthians with holiness and sincerity. Where does Paul claim these attributes originate?

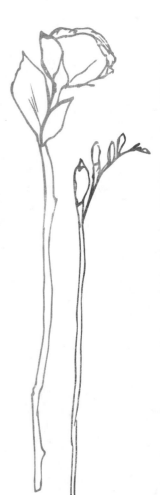

Based on 2 Corinthians 1:12-13,17-19,24, what can you surmise were some of the accusations the Corinthians had against Paul? Make a list.

Before we move too far into the heart of today's passage, let's get our bearings on where we are in the time line of Paul's relationship with the Corinthian church. According to verses 15-16, what were Paul's initial travel plans?

The church had not responded well to 1 Corinthians. Paul's ministry co-laborer, Timothy, had visited the Corinthians after Paul wrote that letter, reporting significant problems—moral issues, corrupted beliefs, and relational factions, to name a few. As a result Paul sailed from Ephesus to Corinth to deal with the Corinthians in person, which he'll refer to in 2 Corinthians 2:1-2 as a "sorrowful visit."

Paul may have told them during this difficult visit that he'd see them again on his trip from Macedonia back to Judea.[9] However, when the Corinthians continued to attack him, it's reasonable to assume he made the decision to not return for a while. You probably can relate to the sadness and frustration of trying to reconcile a difficult relationship when nothing seems to be working. Sometimes you just need distance.

Are you in the middle of a relationship you don't know what to do with? If so, describe it below. My prayer is that the Lord will use this study to give you wisdom and grace in that relationship.

Today's text reveals the Corinthians had questioned Paul's motives for not coming. Although he loved them dearly, a band of opponents had stirred up the Corinthian church, casting doubt about the true and sincere nature of Paul's devotion. Might I insert here that, for me, this is the worst. I hate to be misunderstood, especially in a situation where I've actually bent over backwards, sacrificed, stood up, or went out on a limb for someone. I'm not saying this happens to me often, but when it does I wrestle with two basic decisions: 1. Do I trust the Lord with my reputation, resting in a clear conscience before Him (v. 12)? 2. Can I continue to love those who have accused me?

PERSONAL REFLECTION: *What is your default reaction when you're misunderstood or falsely accused?*

Paul wasn't into mixing his yeses and noes, saying one thing but doing another. According to 2 Corinthians 1:18-19, why was his ministry toward the Corinthians straightforward and trustworthy?

It's usually not meant positively when someone tells you you're being defensive about something. We may think the only godly response is to remain silent and never explain ourselves. (Proverbs 9:8 says not to rebuke a mocker.) But sometimes explaining our actions is not only appropriate, but also vital to the relationship. So how do you know if you should defend yourself or not? Here's a litmus test I use: If defending myself is motivated by self-protection and characterized by pride, anger, fear, or self-righteousness, it's most likely from my flesh. Whereas, if defending myself is motivated by love for the other person and characterized by clarity, humility, kindness, and sincerity, it's from the Spirit. We'll note throughout our letter that Paul was clearly defending himself, not for self-defense's sake, but for the love of the Corinthians.

What reason does Paul give for not having gone to Corinth (v. 23)?

What is Paul working for in verse 24?
The Corinthians' …
❑ *hope*   ❑ *purity*
❑ *security*   ❑ *joy*

Whether we serve as bosses, teachers, mothers, ministry leaders, or have other positions of authority, we could solve a multitude of problems if we worked for the joy of those we oversee. In other words, if we're motivated by power, significance, position, advancement, money, or self-worth, then our leadership is not based on God's love. The people we serve can tell if we're leading them out of our own self-interest or for their joy.

PERSONAL RESPONSE: *How does Paul's gracious response throughout today's text specifically encourage you to respond when criticized or misunderstood?*

I sat with my 80-year-old English friend, Rhona, today. I was commenting on the crossword puzzles she works to keep her mind sharp and how she stays young by traveling and taking care of her grandkids. Her response was pure English, "Oh, but you never know what might strike you!" It's true. Sometimes things strike. Our circumstances can shift and the people we love can drift. Life can float us a few yeses and then slip us a handful of noes. In a world that can feel so unsure, Paul reminds us the ballast of our souls is this: *as surely as God is faithful* (v. 18).

Do you see what Paul is saying? God is not capricious. He doesn't give yeses after a good night's rest and noes when He's in a bad mood. He doesn't trick us by mixing messages. He is faithful. We may know this intellectually, but have we allowed the faithfulness and trustworthiness of God to settle into our hearts? And do we believe that everything that truly matters is "yes" in Jesus Christ? End today by filling in the following phrases however you see fit.

Because God is faithful, He will _____.

Because God is faithful, I will _____.

DAY 4
SINCERE AND STRAIGHTFORWARD

2 CORINTHIANS 1:12-24

Today we're going to dig deeper into the text we studied yesterday. I had to camp out here a little longer because this text holds so much wisdom for us, especially we highly relational women who can occasionally be passive-aggressive, insincere, or codependent—or is it just me? (It's probably just me.) First, let's revisit the word *sincere* in verse 12. Remember Paul explained to the Corinthians that postponing his trip came from a sincere heart. Not because Paul's heart was perfect, but because the sincere love he had for the Corinthians was from God—something he specifically wanted them to know.

I want you to see something really interesting about Paul's use of the word sincere *in an earlier letter. Turn back in your Bible and read 1 Corinthians 5:6-8. What metaphor does Paul use to describe the difference between purity and sincerity versus malice and wickedness?*

The Feast of Unleavened Bread is a festival the Israelites celebrate in remembrance of their deliverance out of Egypt. Ridding their houses of yeast was symbolic of their purity before God. All these years later, Paul was reminding the Corinthian church that a much more insidious yeast needed to be removed, the one in their hearts. This leaven of malice and evil was spilling into conversations and spreading into relationships and poisoning their community. Just as yeast enters a batch of dough and spreads its effect throughout, so does the sin we allow to fester in our thoughts and hearts. Paul was urging the Corinthians and us to get rid of the evil and live with sincerity! (This was way before the gluten-free muffin—Paul was so ahead of his time.)

So, here's a little test I put out to my Bible study group. I'm calling it, "How Sincere Am I?" Respond to each of the following questions with the word that best fits your response: *never, rarely, occasionally,* or *often*. Include any additional thoughts you have to each response.

Do I manipulate the truth to get something I want, avoid a difficult situation, or make myself look better?

Am I straightforward in my commitments and responses so that others know what I'm really thinking?

Do the people around me trust my heart and integrity even when I've hurt them?

Do I often say one thing but mean another?

Can I say my conscience is clear before God?

Sincerity is somewhat of a lost quality in our time, overrun by manipulation, shading the truth, passive-aggressive responses, lying, and flattery. How much richer could the body of Christ be if we were pure and sincere toward one another, as well as to those in the world?

Paul details more specifically what sincerity looks like. Revisit 2 Corinthians 1:17-20. What two small, single-syllable words does Paul emphasize in this text?

In verse 17, what does he say he does not do in the same breath (or simultaneously)?

What does it appear the Corinthians were accusing Paul of being?
❑ *wishy-washy*   ❑ *shady*
❑ *fickle*   ❑ *all of the above*

We may not purposefully tell people yes when we really mean no, or say no when we really mean yes, but each of us do it in more suble ways. We say things like, "No, really, I'm fine," while giving someone the silent treatment. We said yes to our spouse at the altar, but now flirt with a coworker. We claim we've forgiven someone, but punish that person by withholding intimacy. Or maybe we make a commitment to something but carry it out annoyed— essentially saying yes with a huge no in our hearts. Or the opposite—we say no with our words while every other part of our lives is saying yes to what we should be resisting.

A friend of mine who's married and a new mom said this, "When you're married, a lot of times it starts out as less about manipulation or shading the truth and more about keeping the peace and avoiding disagreement. Over time, continuing to just 'keep the peace' may build into silent treatment or a grudge when a brief discussion about the situation would have been the better choice. If we approach the situation with sincerity and honesty, the approach Paul displayed, then we are on the right path in our relationship."

> **PERSONAL REFLECTION:** *Are you in a current situation where your yes is not really yes, or your no is not really no? If so, prayerfully commit to straightening out your yeses and noes in this situation.*

If we stopped here we'd have a really helpful lesson in integrity and forthrightness. But I'm so grateful Paul doesn't stop here because today's study is about so much more than merely upping our integrity meter. Go with me here.

> *Who had Paul and his friends been preaching about to the Corinthians (v. 19)? The _____ of God, _____ _____.*

Do you see that this is not merely a message in trying to do better, but is all about the person of Jesus? Paul goes even further.

> *All the promises that God has made are _____ in Christ (v. 20).*

> **PERSONAL TAKE:** *Why do you think Paul includes this section about God's promises always being "yes" in Jesus as part of his defense to the Corinthians?*

A distinction of the Christian faith is that it's not merely about achieving moral standards or looking like well-behaved Christians for the sake of being really good people. Paul had already spent much of his life in that pursuit, achieving a stellar Jewish education, being a member of the Pharisees, being trained by a top rabbi, and executing self-righteousness flawlessly. But he realized all of his "goodness" amounted to nothing but a dung heap.

More than that, I also consider everything to be a loss in view of the surpassing value of knowing Christ Jesus my Lord. Because of Him I have suffered the loss of all things and consider them filth, so that I may gain Christ.
Philippians 3:8, HCSB

That's literally how he put it in Philippians 3:8.

Now that he is defending his actions to the Corinthians, his point is that being wishy-washy or untrustworthy toward them would go against one of his core beliefs: God is faithful. He cannot lie. He cannot go back on His Word. He made a covenant promise to redeem His children, and every promise included in that is "yes" in Jesus. Jesus is God's yes to His promise to Abraham that by Abraham's seed all the nations in the world would be blessed, and yes to His promise that David's throne would be established forever. And Jesus is God's yes to us for the life of meaning and hope we are longing for.[10] In other words, "For in relation to [Jesus], every last one of God's promises receive 'yes' for an answer."[11] If God is not fickle with His yeses and noes, well, then neither was Paul.

Jesus is God's yes to us for the life of meaning and hope we are longing for.

I wonder if one of the reasons we're not always sincere or straightforward in our relationships is because we're not grounded in the "yes" of Christ. I know I've waffled, and at times manipulated, situations because I've wanted to make my life work the way I wanted it to. Sticking to a yes or no may have threatened that pursuit. But when I'm able to trust God's faithfulness, both His character and rule over my life, I don't have to be manipulative or insincere.

PERSONAL RESPONSE: *As we close today's study, what's been the most convicting part for you? If you can connect it to a specific verse from our text, write the verse alongside what you've learned.*

DAY 5
NOT TO
BE OUTWITTED

2 CORINTHIANS 2:1-11

In the first part of today's reading we'll encounter a situation every one of us has faced: making sad the people we depend on to make us happy. In other words, when we have to confront a friend we love and enjoy, someone we like to go shopping with, and we know this confrontation will make our friend upset, maybe even mad, then who will we have to help us try on jeans? If it's a daughter who needs correcting, how will you deal with being the un-fun mom for a spell? If it's a spouse or boyfriend who's done something particularly hurtful—and you know you need to say something—who's going to take you out to dinner that night? We've all dealt with this dilemma, which is one of the reasons I love the way Paul addresses this scenario.

READ 2 CORINTHIANS 2:1-4.

In your own words, summarize why Paul decided to stay in Ephesus.

According to verse 4, describe the emotions Paul experienced while writing his painful letter. (Note: This sorrowful letter appears to be a lost letter Paul wrote after his difficult visit to Corinth, most likely delivered by Titus.)

For what express purpose does Paul say he wrote this letter (v. 4)?

Holiness is the foundation on which thriving relationships find their footing.

One of the reasons we avoid confronting sin in another person's life is that we've made happiness the chief goal of our relationships—our own or the other person's. But true love shoots much higher than mere happiness. It shoots for holiness, which is not, as we may fear, stiff or boring. Holiness is the foundation on which thriving relationships find their footing.

Whatever sin Paul was addressing in the lives of the Corinthians—sin that was eating them alive (some of which we'll find out in more detail)—he wasn't confronting the Corinthians to hurt them, but rather to let them know how deeply he cared! Perhaps one of the most tragic ways we fail to love someone is when we say or do nothing while they run off the rails, all because we don't want to upset the applecart—usually, our applecart.

PERSONAL REFLECTION: *Briefly write about a time when someone took a risk to lovingly call you out on something, and in doing so, demonstrated his or her deep love for you.*

According to verse 4, Paul wrote not for the sake of causing _____.

Instead, Paul wrote to express his love. In the original language Paul grammatically positioned the word *love* in a way the Corinthians couldn't miss. He had a deep love for them and an equal desire for them to know that he loved them. Goodness, who hasn't felt this way about someone we've desperately wanted to see healed, restored, or delivered? We may love a person deeply, but something may be preventing him or her from knowing it. Paul wanted to make sure the Corinthians knew of his love.

PERSONAL RESPONSE: *You may have someone in your life you long to see free from sin. I wonder if this person interprets your desire as being motivated by something other than love? Even if you've approached him or her in humility, mercy, and kindness, does this person view you as a killjoy or holier-than-thou? Explain. Pause and pray that this loved one will receive your concern and correction as love.*

READ 2 CORINTHIANS 2:5-11.

Before we get into the details of who the person Paul mentioned might be, to whom did this person grieve and cause pain (v. 5)?

Why did Paul advise the church to forgive and _____ him (v. 7)? Fill in the blank and respond.

Some believe the offender in this passage is the man Paul wrote about in 1 Corinthians 5:1-5 who had committed incest. Other scholars disagree because the details in that passage don't seem to match the ones in 2 Corinthians. What we do know is that this specific person had attacked Paul personally, which in turn, affected the whole church community. This man's offense seems to be the focal point of a lot of the heartbreak Paul was experiencing with the Corinthians. Whatever his offense, it was significant.

In response to Paul's directive, the Corinthian church had taken some sort of disciplinary action toward this man, probably removed him from fellowship for a time, but now Paul was calling for his restoration. The discipline had been effective, and now it was time to restore the man to the community.

> **PERSONAL TAKE:** *You've already noted that Paul urged the church to forgive and comfort this person. In verse 8 he tells them to reaffirm their love for him. What do you think this reaffirmation of love looked like and why was this extra step necessary?*

We're about to focus on one of the most powerful words in all of Christendom, a word mentioned several times in verse 10. Write it below.

According to verse 11, what reason does Paul give for offering forgiveness?

> **PERSONAL TAKE:** *Why do you think forgiveness protects us from being taken advantage of or outwitted by Satan? Give this some thought. If it helps you to think in opposite terms, how does not forgiving allow Satan to gain a foothold in our relationships?*

"Forgiveness protects us from the strategy of Satan in our lives."

A friend of mine who's a missionary talked once about forgiveness and 2 Corinthians 2:10-11. He said something so powerful that I wrote it down in the margin of my Bible and return to it often, "Forgiveness protects us from the strategy of Satan in our lives." This, my dear friends, will serve and protect us for the rest of our lives.

READ COLOSSIANS 3:13.

We're to forgive, just as _____.

If you have the extra time, spend a few minutes meditating on Matthew 18:21-35. Here, Jesus gives the example of a servant whose significant debts were forgiven, yet when later put in a position to show forgiveness, mercilessly demanded a much smaller debt be repaid. The point is that when we harbor unforgiveness toward someone, we've started to lose touch with our own need for forgiveness and to lose sight of the forgiveness Jesus has freely given us.

PERSONAL RESPONSE: *Is there anyone you need to forgive? The situation can be current or it could be a wound that happened 30 years ago. The person could be in your home or may not even be alive anymore. If you can't think of anyone, let's go another step. Do you gossip about a particular person or rejoice in his or her misfortunes? If so, this may mean you have a root of bitterness toward that person that can only be dug out through forgiveness. Take the steps needed to extend forgiveness. This may mean a face-to-face conversation, a personal letter, or perhaps just a prayer. Or it could be a combination of these steps. Feel free to use the margin to detail your plan or write your prayer.*

When we don't forgive, teams form, bitterness brews, and division ensues.

When we don't forgive, teams form, bitterness brews, and division ensues. Let's protect ourselves from the strategy of Satan in our lives. Let's reflect on the forgiveness the Lord has shown us and offer that forgiveness to others. Let's forgive, comfort, and reaffirm our love to those who have hurt us. When we do so, we will clearly display the unique power of the Christian faith shown in Scripture: "For he has rescued us from the dominion of darkness and brought us into the kingdom of the Son he loves, in whom we have redemption, *the forgiveness of sins*" (Col. 1:13, emphasis mine).

(Note: While forgiveness is always necessary, there may be some instances where comfort or reaffirmation of love is not appropriate or wise considering the circumstances. Seek the Holy Spirit's leadership and wise, godly counsel in these situations.)

We've had a great first week together. I hope you're excited to keep going. Paul's relationship with the church in Corinth was anything but simple, which is one reason I find it so refreshing. Second Corinthians is a real letter to a complicated group of people much like ourselves, and unless your life is perfectly put together, this is the kind of letter we need.

My hope is that you've already experienced some of the comfort and compassion from the Father of all mercies Paul wrote about in this opening chapter. My desire is that you've placed your hope on this compassionate God like a satchel bearing all of its weight on a single hook. If you find yourself navigating a difficult relationship, perhaps you have leaned on the wisdom Paul used to love, instruct, and correct with good measure and timing. I know you'll do your best to not be easily offended, but when you are, don't allow unforgiveness to lurk in the corners of your heart. We don't want the enemy to outwit us. May we freely give what we've been freely given.

SESSION 2 VIEWER GUIDE

THE GOD OF ALL COMFORT

GROUP DISCUSSION:

Have you ever interpreted your suffering as God's punishment? Based on the teaching, why is this not necessarily the case?

How does it help to know that your suffering has purpose when you're walking through it? Explain.

How has Jesus comforted you in your suffering? And how have you been able to comfort others in their suffering?

Has going through suffering made you more patient? Explain.

How have you learned obedience through suffering?

What one thing stood out for you from this video?

Two-Day Chicken Noodle Soup (serves 8)

INGREDIENTS:	A friend of mine had me over for lunch
1 whole chicken	and served homemade chicken noodle soup
½ pound noodles	her mother had made. I found out my friend's
1 onion, chopped	mother is in her 80s, which is precisely why
1 cup chopped celery	the soup tasted so good. She's boiled a few
6 carrots chopped	chickens in her life. I asked my friend to
¼ cup chopped parsley	email me the recipe, and two days later
salt and pepper to taste	a card landed in my mailbox, stamp and all,
	with a recipe card written in her mother's
	handwriting.
	This, my friends, is the real deal.

DAY 1 DIRECTIONS

Wash the chicken, place in a large pot, cover with water, and boil 50 minutes. Remove chicken and reserve liquid in pot. Remove meat from bone, cut into pieces or shred, and store in refrigerator overnight.

Return bones to liquid in pot and gently boil for one hour. Separate the liquid from the solids by pouring through a sieve. Discard bones. Cover broth and refrigerate overnight. (Store in separate container than chicken.)

DAY 2 DIRECTIONS

Overnight a layer of fat will have risen to the top of the broth. Remove and discard fat.

Cook chopped celery, onion, and carrots in a small amount of water over medium-high heat until soft. Add broth to vegetables and heat through.

Meanwhile, cook the noodles separately according to package directions until al dente. Drain and add noodles to broth. Taste soup and season with salt, pepper, and half the parsley. Stir in reserved chicken. (You may find you have extra chicken for the amount of broth, so add until you're content with the amount of meat in the soup.) Taste again for seasoning. Heat until warmed through. Sprinkle with remaining parsley to serve.

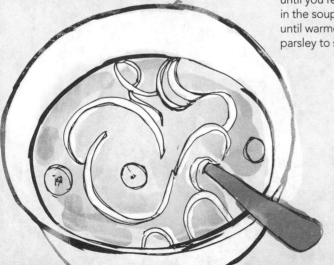

SESSION 3

NEW COVENANT MINISTRY

Cities can be the oddest places. They're this amalgam of every type of creature under the sun converging in one spot for every conceivable activity under the sun. I was reminded of this after speaking at a church's women's retreat a couple of hours outside of Los Angeles. After the weekend, I headed back to the city for a few meetings, one of them in Santa Monica. (Please keep in mind that nearly 100 percent of my travels entail meetings *not* in places on the ocean.) I had the day to walk the beach, the pier, and Third Street Promenade, and let me tell you, Santa Monica has some characters. Some real dramatic folk.

Some of them were in costumes for unbeknownst reasons in the middle of the day. Two roller bladers almost took me off this earth while blazing by me at cheetah speed. One weathered and long-bearded gentleman held a sign that said, "Need money for pot." He was apparently running low. The people stretching on the beach intrigued me, especially the ones who got into particularly interesting positions showcasing their flexibility or soul liberation or things I don't think they should be showcasing. Of course, there were also the businessmen and women, the shoppers, the tourists, the celebrities I never laid eyes on despite my stealthy efforts, and people like me who were simply looking for a place to get frozen yogurt with fresh mango. Upon further thought, I may have been the only person looking for this.

Sheryl Crow was right—pretty much everyone looked like all they wanted to do was have some fun until the sun came up over the boulevard.[1] The only problem was that no one looked all that happy. (This is often true in any city.) It's taken me a lot of years to realize that fun and genuine happiness aren't all that closely related after all, and that all you could ever want is not really all you ever wanted. I strolled the city with a leisurely California gait but inside I felt like I was trying to bat back the waves of heaviness undulating around me with a fly swatter. A sea of people seeking happiness and beachy sunshine, or maybe celebrity status, but didn't look like they'd found it. Or if they'd found it, whatever they now possessed hadn't done the trick.

I considered the good tidings of Jesus' salvation—what we often refer to as the gospel. This city of forlorn faces clearly needed it, as do all cities. Why? Because cities are where the people are.

Over the past few years I've been so stirred for the gospel's good news to get to the ends of the earth. Places like the Amazon and Moldova are two of those passions for

me. But oh how the ends of this earth include the house next door, the Hollywood gated communities, sky-scraping offices we work in, theatre districts, boardwalks, five-star hotels, low-income housing, and everything in between. To be honest with you, this presents a challenge for me; I often feel more at ease sharing the gospel with a hostel of orphans or a remote village in far away lands than I do with a city executive, actress, intellectual, or, for that matter, any one of the beach stretchers. Maybe this is because all these city people are in a sense my people. And ministering to your own people has a way of getting awfully personal.

Ministering to your own people has a way of getting awfully personal.

When I share about my relationship with Jesus in the community I wake up in every morning, I'm opening the package of the gospel in front of the people I live alongside. This is an entirely vulnerable experience. Some think the gospel package is too narrow, others find it offensive or woefully irrelevant. A few really hate what's inside. Most, regardless of how they feel about what's in the box, at least want to know if your life resembles its contents. Maybe this is why Paul puts such an emphasis on the steadfast characteristic of sincerity.

I don't get to drop the news of Jesus off on someone's doorstep and then dash away from the questions and criticisms that people in the city are educated enough to fire at me. And I'm not even talking about the inquiries delivered out of spite. Rather it's questions born from the genuine wounds of kindhearted unbelievers: *Why didn't my child get healed when I prayed? How come Christians are so judgmental? The church really hurt me as a kid. Why would God have allowed my abuse? Why is Jesus the only way? Can't we all just believe what we want and love one another?*

You can see how tempting it is—as the Sunday School song goes—to hide your light under a bushel. Because when you talk about Jesus in the context of the place you live, people start watching you with those interrogating cat-eyes. They want to get to the bottom of all this God-talk. To see if your faith rings true. When hardship befalls our neighbors they want to know what our prayers can do for them. When trials befall us they want to see how we'll walk through the valley. We often wonder, *will I say the right thing? Have the right answer? What if I don't explain the gospel well?*

And then there are the many who are drawn to the life-changing grace of Jesus! Those just dying—some literally—for someone to show up in their lostness as a minister of reconciliation, an ambassador for Jesus. They'll rip into the box with vigor, paper sailing everywhere, like they've been waiting for this good news delivery all their lives. But you know what this means? Hands-on discipleship time. So you still don't get to leave the package and run.

Do you see how personal all this is? How ministry in the city, in your community, in your church, will crawl into every crevice of your life and faith?

This is precisely what I've loved and found challenging in studying 2 Corinthians. Paul and his co-laborers served in Corinth, in the complications of a wealthy, artistic, athletic, and commercial society. The sway of political power was real, and the pull of wealth Herculean. Social status was central to one's worth and intellectualism relentlessly took Paul's spiritual wisdom to task. Every inch of the gospel gets tried and tested in a city like Corinth, just as it does in our cities today (the same can be true in rural and quieter communities, as well). The good news, you ask? God has made you competent for the adventure wherever you live. In your place of community. Where all the people are.

DAY 1
THE FRAGRANCE
OF CHRIST

2 CORINTHIANS 2:12-17

We're about to embark on a short but emotional section of our letter. Scholars have noted that 2 Corinthians is the most deeply personal and passionate of Paul's letters. The opportunity to peer into the raw openness of Paul's dialogue with the Corinthians allows us a unique window into the longings of his heart. We can make the mistake of thinking that since Paul had a personal encounter with Jesus, became an apostle, and wrote a sizeable chunk of the New Testament, he didn't battle loneliness, bruised feelings, or ever feel torn over a difficult decision. However, today we'll see that Paul was exceedingly human, susceptible to the same relational concerns that we are. We'll also find that decisions were not always clear to him—he had to seek and toil as we do.

READ 2 CORINTHIANS 2:12-17.

Where had God opened a door for Paul?
❏ *Macedonia*   ❏ *Rome*
❏ *Corinth*   ❏ *Troas*

True or False: *Paul expected to find Titus there, but when he didn't show up Paul pressed through and ministered by himself.*

PERSONAL REFLECTION: *Have you ever arrived at a place, be it a physical landmark or a season in life, where you were counting on someone to be there for you who wasn't? If so, explain how you felt. What did you do?*

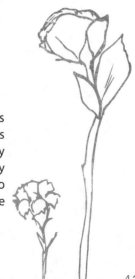

One of the reasons Paul was intent on finding Titus was because Titus had visited Corinth and would be able to tell him how the Corinthians had received his letter. Were they angry? Had they cut him off? Had they repented or retaliated? Were they allegiant to the false teachers, or had they turned back to the true gospel of Christ (2 Cor. 11:1-4), and therefore to Paul as their leader? You can imagine Paul's unrest as he ruminated over the negative and positive scenarios that captivate a mind in waiting.[2]

Paul said in verse 13 that he had no rest in his spirit (or peace of mind). Titus was a younger servant in the faith and someone for whom Paul cared a great deal. It's easy to understand Paul's concern when Titus didn't show up when he was supposed to. Titus's whereabouts may have also been a sign that his recent visit to the Corinthians hadn't gone well, so Paul had several reasons for being troubled.

Can anyone else identify with how nearly impossible it is to concentrate or minister or wash the dishes when your mind is on something else? I had a conversation once with my Aunt Carol Jo about this. "Whenever I'm really upset about something, I just reset," she said.

"How exactly do you reset?" I asked. This was fascinating to me.

"You know, before I go to bed I hit the reset button, she explained. The next day I wake up, and I start fresh."

"Aunt Carol", I persisted, "psychologists have words for this! They call it denial, compartmentalizing, detaching. You can't just reset!"

"Yep, it's what I do", she replied. "It's worked for me for years."

My Aunt Carol Jo has one of the best dispositions the Lord could have doled out to a human being. She has my mom's side of the family's easy-going, not easily ruffled demeanor, and perhaps embedded in that DNA she inherited a reset button. I don't know. All I can tell you is I've never known such a thing. I'm more akin to Paul when upset and preoccupied and can find positively no rest in my spirit.

> *Paul makes a marked leap from having found no rest and leaving for Macedonia in verse 13 to the beginning of verse 14. In the margin, write the first five words of verse 14.*

After verse 13 Paul takes a five-chapter break from this story line, picking back up in chapter 7. This will be important to keep in mind, otherwise the next few chapters will seem out of place. For now, skip to 2 Corinthians 7:5-7 and answer the following:

While we can't be certain that the things Paul was giving thanks for in 2:14 are directly connected to 7:5-7, there's a lot for Paul to be grateful for here. These verses reminds us that God hears the cries of our hearts, especially for our loved-ones. According to these verses (7:5-7), list all the things for which Paul could be thankful.

Perhaps when Paul wrote about leaving Troas for Macedonia it sparked his memory of reconnecting with Titus. It was there in Macedonia that Titus told Paul about the change of heart the Corinthians had toward Paul. While not everything was perfect, a seismic shift had taken place in Paul's relationship with the Corinthians, and he knew all thanks could be directed to none other than God Himself.

PERSONAL RESPONSE: *Write a prayer of thanksgiving for a relationship in your life that God has restored. Or write a prayer asking God to redeem a broken relationship you long to see restored.*

Finish writing out verse 14, which you started earlier in the margin.

We're not from Roman culture and have little context from which to draw when it comes to a Roman procession—I just can't bring myself to use Mardi Gras or Macy's Thanksgiving Day Parade® as comparable examples. So a note about what Paul is most likely referring to here. The Greek word *thriambeuō* means *to be led in triumphal procession*. In Paul's day, the Romans were known for their grand processions that festooned through the streets after a significant victory in battle. Perched on the lead chariot the conquering general dressed in full regalia would have stood, and the spoils from the war would have preceded him. Victorious Roman soldiers— along with the captives who were being led to death—trailed after him.

2 Corinthians 2:14 says, God _____ leads us in triumphal procession.
- ❏ *always*
- ❏ *sometimes*
- ❏ *if we do the right thing*
- ❏ *hopefully*

PERSONAL REFLECTION: *Paul had zigzagged like a nomad all over the place, facing great hardships and uncertainties. Yet he could thankfully and confidently state he was always being led in God's triumphal procession in Christ. How does this truth encourage you in seasons where you can't for the life of you figure out where your life is going or when hardship seems to endure forever?*

As those in the victory march of Christ's triumphal procession, another element is at play. Paul says that through us the _____ of the knowledge of God is spread.

Part of the Roman processional included incense bearers who marched carrying incense baskets and burners that spread the aroma of the victory. I love this imagery because as we go through life Paul reveals that we're constantly spreading the aroma of Christ! Last night I ran into an acquaintance at the grocery store. She cannot stand the idea of Christianity, but she likes me well enough. As we caught up I was praying that I'd be a peaceful presence in her life, a scent that smelled like Jesus even if her heart was opposed. The next aisle over I bumped into a friend who's going through a divorce. She's a believer, and, in like fashion, I hoped to be an encouraging aroma of Christ's presence to her at this heart-wrenching bend in her journey. I ended up in the cheese aisle, which was a different scent altogether, but you understand. Everywhere we go, at all times, we are spreading the aroma of Jesus.

Everywhere we go, at all times, we are spreading the aroma of Jesus.

PERSONAL TAKE: *In your own words, what does the fragrance of Christ look like on a person?*

According to 2 Corinthians 2:15-16, what do the people around us think of the fragrance of Christ?

I find this part troubling. The part of me that wants to be liked, to win friends and be admired, would prefer to wear one surefire fragrance that every person is drawn to. I'd like to know I've got the hit scent all of the time. The sobering reality is that the fragrance of Christ is glorious to those who desire Him as Savior, but to those who have rejected Him, the scent is loathsome. Paul spoke to this in 1 Corinthians.

READ 1 CORINTHIANS 1:18,22-24.

Why is Jesus as Savior and Lord desirous to some and repugnant to others?

Will I unashamedly wear the scent of Christ even when it's unpopular?

Will I unashamedly wear the scent of Christ even when it's unpopular? This is the question. In many circles, to wear the fragrance of Jesus means being labeled exclusive, a hater, myopic, reckless, uneducated, simple-minded, or narrow-minded. Oh, but praise God if in the midst of these accusations we can exude the redolence of Christ with humility and selflessness. You may be in a work or family life situation where the backlash you're enduring for being a Jesus follower feels nearly overwhelming. You're in good company. Did you notice at the end of 2 Corinthians 2:16 that even Paul asks, who in the world is sufficient (or equal) to a task like this?

I believe the answer to his rhetorical question is that none of us are up for this. We're all people-pleasers who want to be liked, or we're prideful and want to be right. Either way, we need God's power to unashamedly stand for His Son. As we close today's study, we'll find that the final verse of chapter 2 gives us a hint as to how this can be done.

> *According to verse 17, what did and didn't Paul do that separated him from so many others?*

Perhaps most of us are not in a position to financially profit from the teaching of God's Word. (This hits closer to home for people with vocations like mine.) But we can subtly profit in other ways. Sometimes we "preach God's Word" to win arguments, tear others down, or feel good about ourselves. Or have you ever used God's Word to control or manipulate an outcome? This is all selfishness profiting in its own right.

> *Paul was reminding the Corinthians that he had not brought the message of Jesus to them out of selfish gain. Instead, he had come with that beautiful word found in verse 17. Write the word in the blank: Paul spoke to the Corinthians before God with_____.*

Paul was preaching Jesus without tricks. Without pride. Without selfishness. With love. With compassion. Sans a hidden agenda. For their good.

What if we, the church, were to proclaim Jesus with hallowed sincerity?

The fragrance of Christ will not be a sweet aroma to all men and women. To some it will be a foul smell of offense because the cross of Christ is an affront to our pride. Paul makes this clear. But what if we, the church, were to proclaim Jesus with hallowed sincerity? I dare say a great many more would be drawn to His love—curious to know what in the world it is we're wearing.

> **PERSONAL RESPONSE:** *I encourage you to close today's study by asking God to make you more sincere, especially as it relates to your sharing Him with others. You never know who around you might be longing to breathe in the fragrance of life.*

DAY 2

WRITTEN ON OUR HEARTS

2 CORINTHIANS 3:1-6

Before we set out to study our text today, remember the Scripture Paul had available to him did not include the full 66 books we study today. I bring this up because throughout 2 Corinthians Paul quotes the Bible, his Bible being the Old Testament. It's fascinating to picture him dipping his ladle into the Old Testament and pouring its contents into new covenant bowls. I'll show you what I'm talking about.

READ 2 CORINTHIANS 3:1-3.

Paul asked the Corinthians if they were looking for letters of

_____.

Paul has desperately expressed to the Corinthians how much he loves them, and yet the beginning of chapter 3 finds him having to reestablish this fact again. Picture the scene: false teachers had infiltrated the church in Paul's absence, having decorated themselves with man-made credentials. They were sowing seeds of discord, attempting to overthrow Paul's claim of apostleship and spiritual authority even though he'd personally planted the church.

Read Acts 18:7-8, which describes an event that took place in Corinth. What did many of the Corinthians do?

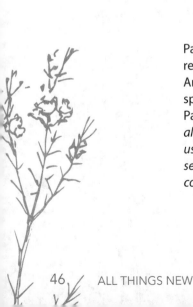

Paul had ministered to Titius Justus, Crispus, and many other Corinthians—real people with names and occupations whom he'd personally led to Christ. And now some of these people were under the sway of self-proclaimed spiritual leaders who were cunningly casting doubt in their minds about Paul. What Paul is saying on behalf of himself and his co-laborers is, *After all we've done for you, are you seriously asking for our resume? Do you want us to rustle up some letters that will vouch for us? I've suffered, I've pleaded, I've served you for free, I've traveled long distances, I've cried over you—what more could validate our positions as God's leaders in your life?*

Back to 2 Corinthians 3:2-3. Who does Paul say are his letters of recommendation?

Read verses 2-3 a couple of times through slowly. List every metaphorical detail given about who the Corinthians are to Paul and his ministry partners.

While working through this study I've often wondered why Paul pursued the Corinthians so passionately and put up with their antics so patiently. I believe one of the reasons is right here in verse 2: the Corinthians were written on Paul's heart. Sometimes we just can't explain the love the Lord gives us for certain people except to say that their lives are like a letter scripted across our very hearts.

The Corinthians were written on Paul's heart.

Now, let's reach back with Paul into his Bible (our Old Testament) and see where he may have been coming from.

> **READ EXODUS 31:18; 32:15-16.** (This is the account of God giving Moses the Ten Commandments for the people of Israel.)
>
> *What were the tablets made of and who had written on them?*

Remember the law and commandments were given to God's people to show them how to live. They were not given as burdens, rather as life-giving boundaries and buttresses. Though they were meant to serve as a blessing, they ultimately couldn't change the heart. Have you ever done or said the right thing while your thoughts were anything but holy? Let's watch how the Lord takes the goodness of the law, plants it in an intimate space, and empowers us to treasure it.

> **READ EZEKIEL 36:26-27.**
>
> *What did the Lord promise to remove?*

What did He promise to give?
- ❏ new heart
- ❏ new spirit
- ❏ His Spirit
- ❏ heart of flesh
- ❏ all of the above

According to verse 27, what would God's people be moved to do as a result of this transformation?

PERSONAL TAKE: *Why was it important for this transformation to take place? In other words, why wasn't attempting to keep the law enough?*

I love how my friend Julie answered this question: "Because we need to be recreated, not just corrected or redirected."

Essentially what Paul is saying is this: *You all want more proof of the integrity of our ministry (letters of recommendation), but don't you see that you are that proof? You're not a ministry project to us that we can check off our list; you're embedded on our hearts! Christ has so dramatically changed your lives that the people around you have taken notice. Unlike the false teachers among you, our ministry to you isn't validated by lifeless ink or based on religiously following rules from a cold tablet, but the work of the Holy Spirit that has transformed your hearts.*

Some of you may be thinking what I've been thinking: The Corinthians don't seem like all that great of an endorsement for Paul's ministry. They're not exactly superstar Christians. Keep in mind that they were new believers who'd responded radically to the message of salvation in Christ. They had a ways to go in their sanctification, but they were Paul's spiritual children nonetheless and had experienced a genuine transformation through Christ.

> **PERSONAL RESPONSE:** *If the Corinthians were Paul's letter of recommendation, to whom is your life a letter of recommendation? In other words, what mentors and leaders in the faith have poured into your life—making you their letter of recommendation? Write the person's name below. And sometime in the next 5 days, take 10 minutes to write that person a note thanking him or her for how his or her ministry has changed you.*

I find myself in transition right now, as though I'm stepping through a threshold from one season to another. With the passage of time I realize I have less people pouring into me and more people looking to me. I'm more frequently the oldest person in the room, the aunt, the big sister, the mentor who's plodded a few more miles than, say, the twentysomethings. This is not to say that no one is giving to me anymore (or that I feel old). I have some of the best family, friends, and church moms who still kiss me on the forehead. I'm just aware that, like a tipping hourglass, the sand is starting to pour in the opposite direction, and it's my turn to pour out.

Sometimes I don't feel ready for this. I'm not sure how to best lead the Bible studies I teach—or the most effective way to express my faith to my unbelieving neighbors. I don't always know what godly advice looks like in complex situations.

> *If you're tracking with me, fill in this statement however you see fit.*
> *"When people look to me, especially on spiritual matters, sometimes I feel*
> *_____."*

READ 2 CORINTHIANS 3:4-6

True or False: Paul's rigorous upbringing in Judaism, his sacrificial lifestyle, and the appearing of Christ to him on the road to Damascus qualifies Paul to find competency in himself.

We discover in verse 6 that our competence is for a purpose. God makes us competent as _____ of the new covenant.

Since studying this passage, I've been reminding myself that my competency to minister and help people comes from the Lord. Anyone who's tried to serve in any capacity—no matter what the role—can relate to being overwhelmed, insufficient, or exhausted. When it comes to effective ministry, we are simply not enough. I hope you'll take time to reflect on how truly amazing it is that God makes us competent ministers by the power of His Spirit.

When it comes to effective ministry, we are simply not enough.

As I ponder the first six verses of chapter 3, I see how innately relational Christian ministry is. Just consider the words Paul chose to describe our sacred calling: letters, hearts, Spirit, new covenant, life. All these words deal with souls and heartbeats, intimacy and connection, life and living. Each one of us is called to be ministers of the new covenant (something we'll study further tomorrow). And this will require us to build relationships that will etch themselves upon our hearts because we will love and be loved deep enough to leave a mark.

We can fear this kind of closeness, though. When someone is written on our hearts and we've boasted about them to others (letters read by everyone), it can be painful if things go south. And when we allow the Spirit of the living God to lead us in relationships, versus just following a list of good rules, we'll have to relinquish control over the outcome. Let's face it, deep relationships require vulnerability, energy, and time, but in the end, relational ministry is the only real ministry there is. And it promises more joy than we could ever hope for.

> **PERSONAL RESPONSE:** *In closing, are you distancing yourself from ministry that requires intimacy? If so, why? And in what way? Spend time confessing this to the Lord and ask for courage to engage others with more of your heart.*

Tomorrow we'll learn more about the old and new covenant, the letter and the Spirit. But for now, I want you to draw encouragement from the truth that our competency as ministers of the gospel does not rest on our abilities, skill sets, brilliance, or likeability, but is found in God. He will give you what you need to serve in the most relational ministry in the world: the ministry of the Spirit.

DAY 3
A NEW MINISTRY

2 CORINTHIANS 3:7-18

The things in which we glory evolve over time. A barefoot toddler on the ocean's shore will marvel at a seashell as he brushes off the sand. When he's a boy he'll beam atop his dirt bike while popping a wheelie, believing there couldn't be anything more spectacular. But one day, chances are, he'll stand nervously at the altar, his gaze locked on his bride at the end of the aisle. As she inches closer toward his hand, nothing on earth will be more glorious than what radiates before him. Perhaps in years to come he'll witness the miracle of his firstborn, then his grandchild, and 50th wedding anniversary. The glory will increase and so will his capacity for it. Something grander than a seashell and a dirt bike will have dawned, but who could have whispered that to the toddler on the sand or the boy on his bike in mid-air?

Glory is a difficult word to describe, but we know it inherently. A western sky at dusk is the glory of the sun. An October tree on fire with hue is the glory of autumn. The face of Christ is the glory of God (2 Cor. 4:6). The Greek word for *glory* is *doxa*, and while difficult to fully describe, can mean "appearance, form ... that appearance of a person or thing which catches the eye or attracts attention, commanding recognition ... splendor, brilliance, glory attracting the gaze...embraces the excellence and perfection of the divine nature."[3] One thing we know for sure is that degrees and increments of glory exist. Today we're going to look at the glory that increased from the old covenant to the new—and will increase until Christ's return.

WITH THIS IN MIND, READ 2 CORINTHIANS 3:6-11.

Two ministries are mentioned in verses 7-9. Paul describes each with two words. Fill in the appropriate word from the corresponding list.
Ministry of death and _____ *(Shame, Fear, Condemnation, Tribulation)*

Ministry of the Spirit and _____ *(Righteousness, Forgiveness, Purity, Joy)*

What accompanied both ministries, even though they are so different from one another? (The word is used several times in vv. 7-11.)

50   ALL THINGS NEW

Referring to yesterday's text, verse 6 further differentiates between the old and new covenant. Fill in the blanks: The letter (law) _____ but the Spirit gives _____.

To pull this together, the ministry of the old covenant was characterized by death, condemnation, and what would ultimately kill us. The ministry of the new covenant is characterized by the Holy Spirit, righteousness, and life. One of the glaring differences between the two ministries is that while the old covenant revealed to us our sin, the ministry of the new covenant brings us a remedy for it.

> **PERSONAL REFLECTION:** *Describe a time when you lived under a sense of condemnation, or an internal "death sentence" that you were powerless to change.*

As I write this study, certain parts of my past are being churned up the way the contents of a soup are spun to the surface when the pot gets stirred. I can't help but think of the sentences of shame I've felt at times, trying to be the good pastor's kid while feebly staving off the wayward passions so many of us struggle with. I knew what a godly Christian life was supposed to look like (the law), but I was woefully falling short of that standard and felt powerless to change (condemnation). You could say I was stuck under the glory of old covenant rules. You may ask, how in the world is the word *glory* attached to feeling hopelessly sinful? This is a great question.

We know from the Book of Galatians that the law (God's perfect standard) is meant to point us to Jesus (Gal. 3:19-26). I can testify that the painful realization of my inability to purify my own heart was glorious because this is what ultimately led me to my Savior—even more glorious. If this is still a bit unclear, let's keep pressing on.

For a better picture of what Paul is describing in today's reading we need to go back to Exodus 34 where Moses stood before the Israelites to deliver the law.

READ EXODUS 34:28-35.

Why did Moses put a veil over his face?

According to 2 Corinthians 3:7 what were the people unable to do? Why?

When Moses came down from Mount Sinai to deliver the Ten Commandments to Israel he was unaware that his face was radiant. But this is what happens when you've been in the presence of the Lord, and He speaks to you.

Can you think of a time when you noted someone's countenance had changed because of an encounter he/she had with Christ?

I've noticed that occasionally, we move so far into a culture of grace that we dismiss the Old Testament law as negative and obsolete luggage to be discarded. Remember that the law God gave to His people distinguished good from evil and instructed them how to live. It set them apart from other nations who could only guess at what was right and wrong. The law God gave was good and accompanied by glory. However, ultimately it couldn't save us.

Why couldn't the law give us life? (See Rom. 8:3 in the margin.)

> For what the law was powerless to do because it was weakened by the flesh, God did by sending his own Son in the likeness of sinful flesh to be a sin offering. And so he condemned sin in the flesh.
> Romans 8:3

To whom was the law supposed to lead us (Gal. 3:21-25)?

I realize that some of this information may seem technical and not immediately practical. But if we're to appreciate the ministry of the new covenant we have to understand how hopeless our situation would be without Christ. We have to feel the weight of coming up short of a perfect standard (old covenant) that by its very nature could not stoop to meet our sinful shortcomings. When we truly grasp this we'll be overwhelmed that God's Son humbled Himself to save us, accomplishing for us what the law never could (Phil. 2:8).

I want you to notice an important word, besides glory, that Paul uses to characterize the old and new covenants. Fill in the blanks below.

Now if the _____ that brought death, which was engraved in letters on stone, came with glory, so that the Israelites could not look steadily at the face of Moses because of its glory, transitory though it was, will not the _____ of the Spirit be even more glorious? If the _____ that brought condemnation was glorious, how much more glorious is the _____ that brings righteousness!

2 CORINTHIANS 3:7-9

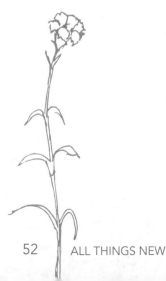

We touched on the word *ministry* in yesterday's lesson, being reminded that God makes us competent as ministers. "The word can be used to speak of 'aid,' 'service,' 'support,' 'an office,' an 'assignment,' or 'mediation.' Paul uses the term for work done in the service of Christ and for Christ's church."[4] I emphasize this word because as followers of Christ we're all called to be ministers of His gospel. What Paul is talking about here isn't mere theology for us to study; it's ministry for us to do. And if we're to be about this ministry we need to know what it looks like. Paul differentiates between Moses' ministry, which relayed a good law that was powerless to change the condition of our hearts, and the new ministry that brings righteousness and life.

So what does this mean for us? To begin with, it means we're not grumpy Jesus-servants lowering the boom on everyone who doesn't measure up to a righteous standard. Instead, we recognize the devastating reality that no one measures up through human effort, yet we tell the glorious truth that through the new ministry of Jesus He measures up for us (Rom. 3:23-24)! It means we're no longer slaves to our lust, jealousy, and pride—Jesus offers us the power to change since ushering in the new—and therefore have a ministry that delivers freedom to those stuck in the prickly briars of shame and failure. It means we're not doling out rules and requirements to everyone, rather we're offering the Holy Spirit who changes us and enables us to love and obey God. Do you see the difference between these two ministries?

> For all have sinned and fall short of the glory of God. They are justified freely by His grace through the redemption that is in Christ Jesus.
>
> Romans 3:23-24, HCSB

PERSONAL RESPONSE: *Though we're not Jews worshiping in synagogues or looking to the Law of Moses as our ultimate hope (as Paul is referencing here), we can still miss the glorious ministry of the Spirit, falling back on our own efforts to fix ourselves. If you're presently trying to achieve your own righteousness, how can you press into the ministry of the Spirit instead?*

According to today's passage, the glory of the old covenant, though good, was temporary, lesser in degree, and unable to fix the human condition of sinful hearts. But the glory of the new covenant ministry is eternal and shines exceedingly bright. Similar to the boy whose bride beams more glorious than the seashell he held as a toddler, the new covenant is more glorious than the old. The new ministry doesn't merely show us what we need to do to become right with God; it makes us righteous.

READ 2 CORINTHIANS 3:12-18.

What does the veil over a person's heart represent?

What is the only way the veil can be removed (vv. 14,16)?

According to verse 12, the new ministry gives us a hope and makes us _____.

When I consider this verse, I realize that to the degree I hope in the good news of Jesus is to the degree I let my testimony shine; to the degree I've lost hope in the gospel is to the degree I put my light under a bushel. This reminds me of a conversation a Christian friend of mine and I had with another friend, Helen, who believes any sincere belief eventually leads to God. In Helen's estimation, if Jesus is the way for you, great, but if it's Buddha or Mohammed, that works, too. I couldn't have been more proud of my friend's unveiled testimony, who in response to this false belief said, "Helen, you know how much I love you." Then with tears in her eyes she continued, "but that is a lie. There is no other way to God except through Jesus." Because only in Christ is the veil removed.

PERSONAL REFLECTION: *How hopeful are you in Jesus and therefore how bold?*

If Moses put a veil over his face to cover his fading glory, Paul says we're to live with unveiled faces to behold God's glory. This is what I want! Peace that transcends understanding, joy in trials, contentment in thin returns, hope when the forecast is bleak, all coalescing in rays of splendor from a bright countenance of one who has beheld His glory.

HEBREWS 9:15 SAYS,

… Christ is the mediator of a new covenant, that those who are called may receive the promised eternal inheritance—now that he has died as a ransom to set them free from the sins committed under the first covenant.

Moses was the mediator of the old covenant, but Christ is the mediator of the new. When we look to Him the veil over our hearts is removed, our sins are forgiven, and a new heart inhabited by His Spirit is granted. Since the veil over our hearts has been removed, let us also pull back the veil over our faces so we can confidently tell others the news that is so gloriously good.

DAY 4
THE TRUTH IN BROAD DAYLIGHT

2 CORINTHIANS 4:1-6

One of the reasons I chose to study and teach 2 Corinthians was because of how personal it is to me. The Holy Spirit used today's portion of Scripture to lead me to where I am now, a place of peace. I couldn't have found this place on my own. Before more fully trusting the Spirit's leading, I followed an inner compass driven by whims, selfish desires, and flawed understanding. Where I intuitively thought peace could be found was often the polar opposite of where it resided. We just can't trust our passions, agendas, or wills unless they line up with God's revealed Word. God has used His Word, over and over again, to redirect my steps to align with His path.

READ 2 CORINTHIANS 4:1-2:

Therefore, since through God's mercy we have this ministry, we do not lose heart. 2 Rather, we have renounced secret and shameful ways; we do not use deception, nor do we distort the word of God. On the contrary, by setting forth the truth plainly we commend ourselves to every man's conscience in the sight of God.

Circle every negative behavior Paul renounces (or doesn't do) in verse 2. You should circle a total of four words.

Of the four negative descriptions, which one has wounded you the most and why?

I want you to see these four words in the original Greek for a clearer picture:

Kryptos: Hidden or secret. Concealed, private, inward.

Aischynē: Shameful. Disgraceful.

Panourgia: Deception. Crafty, cunning, false wisdom.

Doloō: Distortion. Corrupt, ensare, "hucksterize," handle deceitfully. This word "primarily signifies 'to ensnare;' hence, 'to corrupt,' *especially by mingling the truths of the Word of God with false doctrines or notions*, and so handling it 'deceitfully.'"[5]

One of the sure signs we're on the road to captivity is when we think we have to keep something a secret. Keeping confidences is one thing, but whenever we feel a behavior or relationship needs to be kept under cover, not only does this signal a troubling problem in our lives, but it also shows that we're on the road to trading in our freedom. That's the really sneaky thing about sin—it advertises liberty with all its unencumbered fun and seductive sparks, but the moment you bite you're a slave to its rules. Eventually sin requires a tight cover, everything under wraps, nobody can know. Too many people I know are fantasizing about having an affair, getting a divorce because a spouse's affair has finally come to light, or hiding secret things that are bubbling to the surface fracturing otherwise beautiful relationships. So often we can trace things back to an ensnaring sin, which led to shame, which in turn required secretive behavior. This is the enemy's specialty.

Read 1 Corinthians 4:5 where Paul writes about what will happen to the secret things we harbor. What will the Lord do when He comes?

What do Luke 12:2 and Hebrews 4:13 have in common with the verse you just read?

When a person we know or love is keeping something dark or shameful from us but tells us there's nothing going on, it can break our hearts and make us feel positively crazy. Confusion can then brew because we can see the sinful behavior but not know or understand what's prompting it. Rather than go on a witch-hunt or a spree of judgment, we can take great comfort in knowing that God sees the heart. Nothing is hidden from Him. A friend of mine who's going through deep marital pain was recently reminded that God will reveal whatever truth she needs, when she needs it. The heart and secret behavior of my friend's husband may not be laid bare before her, but it's laid bare before God.

Secrecy and shameful ways, deception, and distortion all overlap but they hold their own places of meaning. Something that really jumped out at me was what distortion is attached to in 2 Corinthians 4:1-2.

Paul said he did not distort _____.

Distortion is probably the most damaging one for me. Because I hold God's Word in such high esteem, things can get really confusing when someone twists or uses it to justify a wrong belief or behavior. In the great literary work *To Kill A Mockingbird*, Miss Maudie told Scout, "Sometimes the Bible in the hand of one man is worse than a whisky bottle in the hand of [another]."[6]

Her point was that the Bible carries enormous weight and authority; if recklessly wielded it can cause great harm.

Paul was reacting to the false teachers in Corinth. They were harming the church by distorting God's Word and deceptively covering up shameful behavior, perhaps in the name of Christendom. Paul was saying, *Look, this is not the way my fellow ministers and I have ever treated you.*

Distortion of God's Word plays out in many ways. However, I see two forms most often: bending the Word to either condemn a behavior it doesn't or condone a behavior it doesn't. In Paul's day, the false teachers were twisting the sacred Scriptures to condone whatever greed, immorality, and power struggles they wanted to engage in. The very same thing is happening today and we desperately need discernment from the Holy Spirit and knowledge of the Word to have eyes to see it. On the other side of the coin, when a person in spiritual leadership uses a verse to shame, manipulate, or condemn us where Christ has forgiven, this, too, is just as damaging a distortion.

PERSONAL RESPONSE: *With what do you most identify in your personal experience: the distortion of the Bible to condone a wrong belief or behavior, or the distortion of it to condemn a right belief or behavior? As you think this through, I encourage you to steep yourself in Scripture throughout your life—this is how you'll know when it's being bent to the left or right to accommodate preferences.*

PERSONAL TAKE: *Paul's ministry to the Corinthians wasn't only expressed by an absence of negative behavior but also by the presence of good character. In your own words, paraphrase Paul's statement that begins with "On the contrary ..." from 2 Corinthians 4:1-2.*

Who was Paul's ministry in the sight of?
❏ *Paul's inner conscience*   ❏ *the Corinthians*
❏ *God*   ❏ *the law of the land*

PERSONAL REFLECTION: *Have you ever uselessly tried to get another person (or group of people) to approve of you? Explain.*

How does Paul's declaration that he ministered to the Corinthians in the sight of God free you to live and minister transparently before Him, rather than seeking the approval of others?

If we can absorb this into the core our beings, our lives will take a turn for peace. Too often I've strained to live my life for the approval of others, rather than live openly before God. But this is changing. I still care what people think, but I'm more concerned with what God thinks. I'm finding this to be a more peaceful way of life, even if it means being misunderstood at times.

My friend Julee is a new mom. In response to this passage, she said, "The freedom to live before God and not for the approval of others has become even more important to me than before. It's common for moms to feel pressure from others to do certain things and raise their kids a certain way. This is what makes the freedom to live before God even more essential."

READ 2 CORINTHIANS 4:3-6.

Even though Paul is living with a clear conscience in front of others and in the sight of God, not everyone acknowledges this. What explanation does Paul give for why people don't always see gospel light in our lives (v. 3-4)?

From yesterday's reading, what is the only way people will be able to see this light (2 Cor. 3:14)?

For we are not proclaiming ourselves but Jesus Christ as Lord, and ourselves as your slaves because of Jesus.
2 Corinthians 4:5

According to 2 Corinthians 4:5, what does Paul preach to the Corinthians and why do you think he emphasizes this?

I have a note card with this verse written on it leaning against my desk lamp. When I sit down to write, these words look back at me. Why? Because it can be easy to preach myself and so hard to be a servant. We live in a celebrity culture where an obsession with self, pride, notoriety, and fame is ubiquitous, even in Christian ministry. While I am not immune to this struggle, I experience great freedom when my heart's desire is to share Jesus devoid of worry and concern about myself. It's like dropping 50 pounds worth of self-awareness off your back. It's grand.

As Paul presented his case before the Corinthians, he continually pointed back to Jesus. It would have been easy for him to rest on his good conscience or upright ministry. But he doesn't set forth his wit, charm, or goodness. Only Christ.

PERSONAL REFLECTION: *Are there any relationships or areas in your life where you're "preaching yourself"—places where you are the focus and your agenda is paramount?*

I want to end with what appears to be bookends in Paul's writings.

> *Compare 2 Corinthians 3:7 and 4:6, and check the common word that is connected to both Christ and Moses.*
> ❏ *power*　　　　　　　❏ *face*
> ❏ *radiance*　　　　　　❏ *countenance*

In Day 2 of this week's homework ,we read about how God's people couldn't look at Moses's face because of the glory that shone so bright from him. This glory was in relation to God giving the law to the people through Moses. The law was insufficient in its ability to save, but glorious nonetheless. But now a far greater and brighter glory has arrived in Jesus. Logically speaking, if the Israelites couldn't look on Moses' face that had a fading and lesser glory, how in the world can we look at the face of Christ whose glory is eternal and incomprehensible? Because of the work of Jesus on the cross, the veil has been removed. Because of the ministry of the Spirit that brings righteousness (2 Cor. 3:8-9), we are now able to behold the glory of God in the face of Jesus because our sin no longer impedes our ability to draw near to Him.

I want you to know that no matter where you have been, what you have covered up, or what you are struggling with, you have access to the glory of God. Just this morning I was reminded from Hebrews 10:19-25 that we're able to draw near to God, not because He turns a blind eye to our sin, but because His Son's blood was shed for us on the cross and our consciences have been washed clean. Will you repent of whatever deceit, distortion, shameful, or hidden ways you're harboring, then look anew at the face of Christ? It's where all the glory is.

No matter where you have been, what you have covered up, or what you are struggling with, you have access to the glory of God.

DAY 5

FIXING OUR
EYES ON JESUS

2 CORINTHIANS 4:7-18

We're nearing the end of the week, and, as it turns out, we'll be closing with a passage of Scripture that will prove a balm for the sun-scorched and heavy-laden. If you've wondered what your pain is worth or if any plausible purpose could accompany your sufferings, or if you're hurting so deeply you're not sure you care either way, well then—these verses.

READ 2 CORINTHIANS 4:7-18.

On my desk sits a burgundy leather King James Bible, a weighty gavel of a book as opposed to the light and airy editions that can slip in your purse. My youth group leaders gave it to me on my sixteenth birthday, making it older than I wish it were. I just slid it out from underneath a pile of books and commentaries, opening it for a moment of reflection, because sometimes the best way to reach back into personal seasons of pain is to find the Bible you carried while you traversed them.

Sometimes the best way to reach back into personal seasons of pain is to find the Bible you carried while you traversed them.

PERSONAL RESPONSE: *Reflect on a past trial or the one you're currently walking through. Then, read 2 Corinthians 4:7-18 again. What truth from this passage ministers to you most and why?*

The imagery in 2 Corinthians 4:7 is particularly poignant for me. I often feel inadequate and weak in ministry and relationships, wishing I could be a stronger, more put-together vessel for the Lord to display His power. But Paul says we hold the treasure of knowing Christ in a clay jar, which was a ubiquitous vessel of the time. Ordinary, fragile, and commonplace. This metaphor points to our weakness and fragility but not to our insignificance, as we'll see more clearly in chapter 13.

PERSONAL TAKE: *Look again at verse 7. Why is it important that the treasure of Christ's light is housed in weak vessels?*

The Corinthians had accused Paul of not being a true apostle because of his suffering and weakness. Their thought process probably went something like this: *If Paul is really God's man why is he such a poor speaker? Why is he not wealthy? Why does he suffer so much?* You may be going through a hardship or struggling with certain weaknesses. And it may be easy to think that if God really has His hand on you, you wouldn't be hurting so much and certainly you'd be stronger than you are. But herein lies the great mystery: It's through our weakness that the power of Christ shines most brightly. Dear struggler, don't berate yourself for being an earthen vessel; rather rejoice that the light of Christ is most brilliant in your weakness. The Lord knows the fragility of your frame (Ps. 103:13-14).

It's through our weakness that the power of Christ shines most brightly.

PERSONAL REFLECTION: *Through what weak point in your life have you seen Jesus shine the brightest?*

In verses 8-9 Paul generally describes some of his extraordinary trials, yet an important conjunction follows each one. The word *but*. The suffering Paul experienced was limited in what it could ultimately do to him.

Draw a line between the corresponding statements.

Hard pressed, troubled, pressured, afflicted	But not destroyed
Perplexed	But not abandoned, forsaken
Persecuted	But not in despair
Struck down	But not crushed

Which one of these couplets means the most to you and why?

For instance, right now I'm perplexed about a certain situation that's somewhat painful and difficult for me to understand. But I can honestly say I am not in despair over it because the Lord has given me encouragement and peace.

When it comes to the pain we experience, we may not always consider how it will ultimately minister to others. Furthermore, how often do we consider whether or not the life of Jesus is being revealed through our suffering? Most of the time we're just trying to make it through. But Paul desperately wanted his suffering to bring life to the Corinthians. He wanted Jesus to be revealed to them in his body (weakness). And in verse 15, he says it was all for their benefit! This is others-centered to the hilt, and you get the distinct impression it was his joy.

Let's sum up Paul's view of suffering from verses 10-12: The highest desire in the midst of our suffering is for Jesus to be revealed in us, for the sake of others, for the glory of God. This is not the full scope of the purpose of suffering, nor does it include the way Jesus meets us in our suffering. However, this is a powerful encouragement: If we're going to walk through the valley, it's a blessing to know it will count for God's kingdom and His people.

If we're going to walk through the valley, it's a blessing to know it will count for God's kingdom and His people.

Take another look at verse 13—"I believed, therefore I spoke." This is a quote from Psalm 116:10. Paul's declaration of the gospel was what had caused the persecution he was going through. But just like the psalmist he quotes, who had also been through an intense season of suffering, he cannot help but declare his faith. Essentially, we cannot help speak what we believe, and the more we believe the more powerful our speech.

PERSONAL REFLECTION: *When it comes to sharing your faith, how confident is your belief in the power of the gospel and how often are you speaking about it? Put a dash on each line below on a scale of 1 to 10:*

Degree of faith

|---|
1   10

Degree of sharing your faith

|---|
1   10

We simply cannot have a vibrant faith in Jesus and say we're too private to talk about it. I believe too often we don't share our faith because we're not convinced of the power of God to change lives through the gospel. Perhaps we've grown cynical or our belief has waned in the midst of a trial. I've been asking the Lord for a deeper and more confident faith in Him because the reality is, we can't help but speak what we're unshakably convinced of.

We simply cannot have a vibrant faith in Jesus and say we're too private to talk about it.

Dear friends, I can't think of a better way to end our week than with verses 16-18. Will you stroll through them once more with me? As a result of everything we've studied today, Paul says at the beginning of verse 16, Therefore (fill in the rest) _____.

I recently had one of those big birthdays, and it wasn't 21. As much as I'm trying to lay off the additives and sugar, stretch and exercise, drink stuff like kefir®—which is like pouring yourself a cold glass of bacteria—my body is aging. I can only do so much despite the promising commercials, but trust me, I'm trying.

Even though we are outwardly aging, as believers, what is happening inside our souls on a daily basis? We are being ...
❏ *changed*   ❏ *blessed*
❏ *empowered*   ❏ *renewed*

PERSONAL TAKE: *All of us have either been through or witnessed profound suffering that seemed to go on forever. How is it that Paul can call his suffering light and momentary?*

I love how one scholar says that our trials are producing for us an eternal tonnage of glory that is breathtaking and immeasurable![7] Our sufferings are anything but in vain. As we limp through them, they mysteriously achieve a glory for eternity so vastly staggering we will strangely view our most perplexing and enduring struggles as but a feather's weight that fell upon us but a moment. This is not to passively dismiss the very real pain and devastation so many are going through—Paul himself has taken great pains to list his profound sufferings and will continue to. His encouragement is that no matter how deep the pain drives us here on earth, it will one day explode into breathtaking glory in the other direction, in exponential amount, without end. For us.

Yes, it is all about Jesus shining through our weakness, for the benefit of others, to the glory of God. But in verse 17, Paul lets us know it's also for us, too. I'm thankful the Lord doesn't forget or dismiss our very real pain. For us, He's preparing an eternal glory.

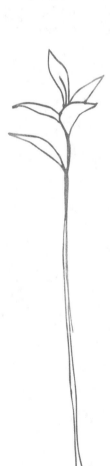

> *Given all of this, we are to fix our eyes on what is unseen, not on what is seen. Because, what is seen is _____ and what is unseen is _____ (v. 18).*

PERSONAL REFLECTION: *We've covered a lot of ground today that also happened to hit us in places that are personal and possibly raw. Write about the most meaningful and/or helpful truth you discovered today and how it has changed your perspective on your suffering.*

You're a third of the way through 2 Corinthians! You've plowed some heavy and, at times, theologically complex ground. I'm so proud of you! This letter is not particularly light, but if we apply what we've learned, we'll find it immensely practical. Just this week I've had to further accept my jar-of-clayness, if you'll allow me to make up a term. I've had to remember that Christ shines brightly through me even in seasons where I'm perplexed or hard-pressed. I've been reminded that the ministry of the new covenant is highly relational, and when this becomes overwhelming, I'm encouraged that my competency is found not in myself but in God. I'm challenged to share my faith more boldly and more often, to let more people know what I believe and why I believe it—to pull back the veil from my countenance since Jesus has taken it off my heart. I've been encouraged to see my struggles and longings in light of eternity, knowing as I surrender them to the Lord, He's investing their momentary existence into an eternal tonnage of future glory.

SESSION 3 VIEWER GUIDE

A NEW MINISTRY

GROUP DISCUSSION:

You may not be in full-time ministry, but how has today's teaching shown you that we're all ministers?

What is it important that we not lose sight of people's hearts as we minister? How can we guard against that?

How does God equip us for ministry? Share a specific example of how God has equipped you in the past or is currently equipping you to be a minister of the new covenant.

Paul states that boldness goes hand in hand with being an effective minister of the new covenant. What specific fears keep you from being bold?

What kind of freedom do we experience in the Lord? If we have this freedom, why do we often live bound and defeated?

What one thing stood out for you from this video?

The music featured in this session is from Kelly's Hymns & Hallelujahs *CD. Video sessions and the CD are available for purchase at* LIFEWAY.COM/ALLTHINGSNEW

Thanksgiving is perhaps my favorite meal of the year. I simply love turkey, but for some reason I don't sit down to a 20 pound bird all that often. This is how ground turkey has made its way into my life. It's lighter than ground beef, but still wonderfully full of flavor. This recipe is great for families or dinner parties. Create a beautiful presentation by serving the meatballs on one platter, the pasta on another. Add warm, crusty bread and a salad or green vegetable.

Turkey Sage Meatballs with Spaghetti (serves 4)

SAUCE INGREDIENTS:	MEATBALL INGREDIENTS:
1 tablespoon olive oil	1 pound ground turkey
1 onion, diced	½ cup parmesan cheese, grated
4-6 cloves garlic, minced	(plus more for garnish)
¼ cup tomato paste	½ cup breadcrumbs
1 (28 ounce) can whole peeled tomatoes	4-5 sage leaves, chopped
in sauce, roughly chopped	4 basil leaves, chopped (plus more for garnish)
1 teaspoon red pepper flakes	1 egg, lightly beaten
2 teaspoon dried oregano	salt and freshly ground pepper
6 fresh basil leaves, chopped	2 tablespoons olive oil (or more)
salt and pepper to taste	1 pound angel hair pasta

SAUCE DIRECTIONS

In a large saucepan or Dutch oven, warm olive oil over medium heat. Sauté onion until translucent, about 5 minutes. Add garlic and cook for 2 more minutes. Add tomato paste, stirring around until slightly browned, about 3 minutes. Add tomatoes, red pepper flakes, oregano, salt, and pepper. Bring to a low boil, and reduce to a simmer. Add basil and stir. Simmer for 45 minutes to an hour, stirring occasionally.

NOTE: If you don't want to go to the trouble of making your sauce, simply pick up a 24-ounce jar of your favorite tomato sauce at the grocery store.

MEATBALL DIRECTIONS

Place the ground turkey, Parmesan, breadcrumbs, sage, basil, egg, salt, and pepper in a large bowl. Use your hands to combine the ingredients and form into 2-inch balls. Heat olive oil in a skillet and brown meatballs in batches over medium heat on all sides until crisp. Cook several at a time, but don't overcrowd the pan. Add olive oil as needed for each batch. Drop the meatballs into the simmering sauce to cook through, about 15 minutes.

Meanwhile, cook pasta according to package directions. Drain and transfer to a platter. Place meatballs and sauce on another platter, and top with fresh basil and Parmesan cheese. Allow guests to serve themselves.

SESSION 4

THE NEW HAS COME

My friends Mike and Patricia used to live in the southern part of Brazil where they started a remarkable ministry for kids. One delightful February afternoon on the Amazon's Rio Negro (delightful is code for molten humidity), Mike and I were having an intriguing chat. We were discussing the challenge, particularly prevalent in developing societies, of motivating people toward a goal they see no reason to attain. He told me about a little known village he'd come to discover that sat in the middle of a mango plantation. The trees dripped with more mangos than the people could possibly consume. The branches bowed with bright and bulbous fruit dangling by slender stems like oversized Christmas lights strung through the village. The sight could make a California fruit stand jealous.

Most of the people in the village had a form of shelter over their heads and just enough food to scrape together for the day's needs. A speared fish for dinner, a helping of manioc, and a peeled mango fresh off the tree could round out a plate. But their plight was meager at best. Poverty ruled the day even in the midst of clusters of mangos that with a bit of ingenuity could be sold for significant profit. But most went uneaten, hurling to the ground, rotting in the heat, and eventually seeping back into the soil.

Mike suggested the village create a dehydration operation that could produce dried mangos, then export them to other parts of the country. The place was a business opportunity just waiting to be pounced on. If the people could just capitalize on the natural resources they were sitting on—or more literally sitting under—they could produce revenue, leading to opportunities for their children, storehouses for lean times, and generally a far better life. Mike saw this not only as a potential escape from poverty, but also a means to prosperity, a route he longed to see the people choose.

When he presented his idea to several of the leaders in the community the response was generally the same, "Why would we want to do that? Why would we want more than what we have?" Their paucity of desire had nothing to do with lack of smarts or ability, rather lack of exposure and vision. They had no picture in their minds of what life could look like other than the one they knew—an existence peppered with disease, alcoholism, and boredom that stems from poverty, and characterized by a lack of education. This was acceptable to them because what else was out there? Industriousness and entrepreneurism seemed like silly ideas because why go to all that trouble when you've already got a mango in your hand?

As Mike told the story, my inner American capitalist was hopping up and down, anxious for this village to see what they were missing. Putting the numerous mangos to work for a better life was far superior to one mango tiding you over until the next meal. That was when the Holy Spirit surprised me with a little illustration, a tutorial, if you will—He's so good at these, and springs them on me when I least expect it. Almost instantaneously, as if staring into a mirror, I saw myself reflected in the people Mike was portraying. I'm far too easily satisfied with the familiar temporal pleasures right in front of me, often at the expense of the lasting and more satisfying pleasures from feeding upon Christ. I find my delight in worldly stuff even though Jesus told us we're to store up treasures that will last and not spend our precious moments on earth for what is fading like a stem that's just been cut. The path of least resistance, though, is to just get by. We're content to live from one fleeting pleasure to another, or in other words, mango to mango. Like the village in Brazil, we are made for exceedingly more but it requires faith to live for the more we have yet to see.

It requires faith to live for the more we have yet to see.

Just because we've yet to behold heaven, doesn't mean we shouldn't live in view of it. This week we'll discuss a world we haven't been to yet, one Paul calls by the most anchoring word my heart knows: home. He writes poignantly about being away from this body and being at home with the Lord. And as our eyes are opened to this unseen world and the Savior who reigns in it, we'll want to live our lives here in view of what will be. We won't be satisfied with the lean pleasures that make promises today but wither tomorrow. We'll know and trust the Word when it says that a life far superior is not only to come but can be grasped right now in communion with Christ.

As C.S. Lewis put it, "It would seem that Our Lord finds our desires, not too strong, but too weak. We are half-hearted creatures, fooling about with drink and sex and ambition when infinite joy is offered us, like an ignorant child who wants to go on making mud pies in a slum because he cannot imagine what is meant by the offer of a holiday at the sea. We are far too easily pleased."[1]

I don't want to be too easily pleased. And by virtue of the fact that you're digging into 2 Corinthians, I don't think you want to be either. This week we have the opportunity to have our eyes opened to a glimpse of what's to come. We'll be reminded that each of us will give an account for how we live our lives on earth, but this doesn't have to be a fearful thing. As we invest our lives for Jesus Christ on this earth—enduring hardship with joy, boldly sharing our faith, generously giving our money and time to those in need, serving in our local church, opening up our homes— we'll be doing so in light of an immutable promise: He has gone to prepare a place for us exceedingly superior to anything we've seen or can imagine. May we not be too easily satisfied with the stuff we can see, simply because it's all we know. More than mangos are ripe for the harvest.

DAY 1
HOME

2 CORINTHIANS 5:1-9

I've suddenly become acutely aware of things I didn't used to think about. Like how difficult it is to bend down a bunch of times while picking up the house, or the shady half-moons under my eyes when I wake up in the morning and a forehead that folds into creases when I do things like smile. All this stuff is making me a little sad, as if my best bodily years are behind me. I'm trying to slow this whole train down but it seems to be oddly picking up speed. And even when I find a great concealer or vitamin supplement, the reality is that it may help me look better for my age, but it won't make me look seventeen. No one's got that pill.

So there's my confession. I don't love this "outwardly ... wasting away" that we closed with last week. I'm all for the inward renewal of the spirit; I just wish I could get both body and spirit tracking in the same positive direction. In a sense, this will one day happen, but instead of the body evolving over time into a superior vessel, it will be redeemed in a moment, totally glorified without an exercise program to achieve it. If you can at all relate to an aging or even ailing body, this study will be especially enlightening and encouraging. And if you're too young to relate—with all your natural beauty and supple skin—just enjoy your youth and tuck this away. It will come in handy one day.

As you read 2 Corinthians 5:1-5, keep in mind the following definitions:

- Earthly tent = physical body
- Eternal house/building (not built with human hands) = resurrection body
- Nakedness = soul without a body
- Clothed = soul with a body

If you got lost in the maze of Paul's mix of metaphors—tents, buildings, clothing, nakedness—you're not alone. Scholars have debated for years some of the nuances of his meanings and intentions here. The main question is, when do we receive our "building from God," our resurrected bodies? One view is that this transformation takes place immediately upon death. A second view is that we receive our resurrected bodies upon the return of Christ. That means that when we die, we go to be with the Lord, but we exist in an unspecified state until Christ returns. While there are good arguments for both views, Paul is not clear. What is clear, from this passage and others, though is that followers of Christ, upon their death, will immediately be with Christ and, at some point, receive a glorified body. So while differing viewpoints exist, the good news is that the gist of his overall message isn't lost.

Paul's main purpose here isn't to describe heaven in detail, but to encourage believers that a real transformation will happen in life after death. In addition, Paul wanted to show his accusers that the suffering he was going through didn't disqualify him from being an apostle—Paul's (and our) ultimate deliverance is yet to come. Yes, we have frail jars-of-clay bodies in this life, but we will one day receive an eternal glorified body.

True or False: Paul begins chapter 5 with uncertain hopes for the resurrection body believers in Jesus will one day receive.

PERSONAL TAKE: *Why would Paul use the imagery of an earthly tent to describe our physical bodies (your version may say "dwelling" but go with tent)? List every reason you can think of.*

PERSONAL REFLECTION: *Given that Paul likens our bodies to tents, I want you to take inventory of how much time, energy, and money you put into your physical body. This includes thinking about body image; clothes and makeup shopping; browsing fashion websites and blogs; working out; getting facials, massages, manicures, and pedicures; hair cuts and colors; having your teeth whitened; going to the spa; seeing a nutritionist; doctor visits; researching essential oils and anti-aging techniques. These are not bad activities, but in excess they can cause us to live solely for the temporal. When our bodies become our focus, we stand to lose our eternal perspective. I want you to underline what three things listed above take up the bulk of your focus, then briefly explain why those three are most important to you. As we learn about our eternal home and body in today's study, ask the Lord to show you if your focus has become out of balance.*

1

2

3

HEBREWS 11:8-10 SAYS,

By faith Abraham, when he was called, obeyed and went out to a place he was going to receive as an inheritance. He went out, not knowing where he was going. By faith he stayed as a foreigner in the land of promise, *living in tents* with Isaac and Jacob, coheirs of the same promise. For he was looking forward to the city that has foundations, whose architect and builder is God. (HCSB, emphasis mine).

Tents aren't that complicated to set up or tear down and they're temporary in nature. Abraham and his family were longing for the permanent dwelling place they knew the Lord had promised to them. In the meantime, they were going to keep things as simple, flexible, and unattached as possible. In the same way, we're to take great care of the earthly bodies God has given us, but we can never lose sight of our permanent home where we'll be with Christ.

> *In 2 Corinthians 5:2, Paul says we _____, longing to be clothed with our heavenly dwelling.*
> ❏ *hope*   ❏ *wish*
> ❏ *groan*   ❏ *pray*

The Greek word for *groan, stenazō,* doesn't have quite the negative connotation here we may think of. Paul says we groan in a hopeful, anticipatory, eyes-scanning-the-dark-horizon-for-the-sunrise kind of way. Paul's groaning wasn't a despairing moaning and groaning. His groaning was based on an absolute, unshakable confidence that we will one day get new bodies that won't be betrayed by age, accidents, or ailments. Far more important, he was groaning for total and perfect unity with Christ.

Here's what I'm wondering: are we doing the wrong things with our groaning? What I mean is, as our outward beauty fades and our bodies tire or become sick, does our groaning propel us toward a bunch of earthly remedies as the ultimate answer, or does it push us into a deeper pursuit of Jesus and a hope for what's to come? I want it to be the latter!

> *According to verse 3, when we're clothed we will no longer be*
>
> _____.

I can't help but think of Adam and Eve after they sinned by eating from the fruit of the tree of the knowledge of good and evil (Gen. 3:7).

> *What were they made instantly aware of?*

Then the eyes of both of them were opened, and they knew they were naked; so they sewed fig leaves together and made loincloths for themselves.
Genesis 3:7, HCSB

Ever since humanity sinned we've been looking to clothe ourselves. Just as the fig leaves were inadequate to cover Adam and Eve's nakedness, our attempts to cover our shame are never enough. Our salvation through Christ manifests itself in so many ways, but being clothed is one of the most meaningful to me. How can we resist the sacrifice of His blood washing us clean, His robes of righteousness covering our shame? Since we are a new creation in Christ (2 Cor. 5:17), this covering is a reality now, though it exists in a failing body. That's why we groan. We are "longing to be clothed … with our heavenly dwelling" (2 Cor. 5:2).

LOOK UP 1 CORINTHIANS 15:53-54.

The perishable/corruptible must be clothed with the _____.

The mortal must be clothed with the _____.

Turn back to today's text and look at the second half of 2 Corinthians 5:4. Keeping this verse and the verses you just read in 1 Corinthians in mind, what does it appear will happen to the body we have now?

When the Lord clothes us with our heavenly bodies, notice He won't destroy the ones we have for the new ones. This is significant; Paul's desire isn't to be rid of an earthly body, but rather to have that body swallowed up by an eternal and immortal one. This truth encourages me to value and take care of my earthly body while simultaneously not putting my final hope in it because I know one day it will literally be engulfed by a new one.

According to verse 5, how can we be certain that we will not be left naked and that our earthly bodies will eventually be completely robed in new bodies?

We long to know that in a world of questions and disappointment, there are anchors of certainty—especially when it comes to what will happen after we physically die. This is why I can't overstate how incredible it is that God has given us His very Spirit as a deposit to guarantee what is to come (2 Cor. 1:22; 5:5). The Lord did not owe us a deposit. He did not have to guarantee us anything. But He knew we'd suffer in this life, as Paul was suffering. He knew we'd question His promises when things start to unravel. He knew our faith would wane when an agnostic professor used empirical evidence to seemingly throw out the foundation of our faith. The Lord knew we would need something certain on which to grasp, for us to make it. So, He gave us a deposit: His Spirit.

PERSONAL REFLECTION: *How has the Holy Spirit acted as a deposit of God's future redemption in your life? Think of specific instances where you knew beyond a shadow of a doubt He was with you and living inside you.*

FINISH READING TODAY'S TEXT, 2 CORINTHIANS 5:6-9.

Being at _____ in the body means being away from the Lord.

Being at _____ with the Lord means being away from the body.

What is Paul's goal no matter where he is calling home (v. 9)?

I've often written about my affinity for the home. For me, friends gathered by the fireplace in winter or around the grill in July are what my friend Karen calls the "rosy moments" of life. The home is an anchor, harbor, place of respite, which may be why we pore over websites that show us how to do home better or make it more inviting. We may not all have the same fondness for cooking, decorating, or hosting, but who doesn't long for home? When we think of home we often think of a physical place, like our house. But what would home be without a sense of community and belonging? In reality, home is not so much about a structure but the people that inhabit it. Did you notice that when Paul describes what it means to be truly home he doesn't point to a place but a person? With the Lord. This is home.

Home is not so much about a structure but the people that inhabit it.

Paul goes so far as to say that if given a choice, he'd leave his body right now to experience the fullness of face-to-face relationship with Christ. I think one of the reasons we're afraid to think too deeply about eternal life is because we're not intimate enough with the Lord now for thoughts of heaven to really be a comfort to us. We prefer to find our comfort in what's cozy and familiar here on earth. But Paul says home is all about where Jesus is. One of my friends recently said this about her understanding of intimacy with God: "I understood God is our Father and loves His children, but I never fully understood that God wants to be in relationship with us—until my 40s." My friend discovered that her true home had more to do with a relationship with Jesus than she'd ever imagined.

PERSONAL RESPONSE: *When you think of all that the word* home *means to you, how much does the presence of Jesus factor into that? In other words, is He your ultimate sense of security? Is He your hope in trials? Is He the one you can't wait to thank in blessing? Do you run to Him first in times of anxiety? Journal your thoughts below.*

CLOSE TODAY BY READING JOHN 14:1-4.

My friend Jessica shared this great insight about this passage, "What I love about this verse is that it's in present tense—there 'are' many rooms. Not, 'there will be once we finish up; we hope to have it done before you get here.' There are. My home is already ready for me."

Jesus tenderly spoke these words to His disciples near the end of His days on earth. Even though a house isn't the only element in creating a home, we sure love an actual structure with a front door: *In my Father's house are many rooms.* He would no longer be with them in the flesh, but He would give them His Spirit as a deposit: *Don't let your hearts be troubled.* The Spirit would be a comfort that would give us confidence: *Trust in God.* As you close today's study, consider that Jesus' words in this passage were all about relationship: *I will come back and take you to be with Me.* Taking us to be with Him. Us with Him. This, dear friends, is the home we've always longed for. And when we get there we'll be swept across the threshold in the bodies we're now in, except they'll be totally new.

DAY 2
A COMPELLING LOVE

2 CORINTHIANS 5:10-15

I grew up in a Christian culture where holiness and Christian behavior were emphasized. Grace was a vital part of the conversation when it came to what it took to get to heaven, but it wasn't talked about as much when life got messy or just plain sinful. Usually those situations just meant consequences. In an effort to right the wrongs of the grace-for-heaven-only mentality, I've seen the church swing perhaps too far in the other direction, where it's all grace at the expense of holiness or obedience. We've become so used to depravity that we're not all that bothered by it anymore. Sin just isn't what it used to be.

A proper tension exists here, doesn't it? We need grace all day long, and certainly there is forgiveness of sins and remarkable redemption of our pasts. However, living without restraints under the premise of grace is to miss its gift. We don't talk about it much, but we will all stand before the judgment seat of Christ and give an account for how we lived our lives. Rest assured that if you're a believer in Jesus this judgment seat has nothing to do with your salvation—that is Jesus' gift and is by grace and grace alone. Still, we need to know that we will be held accountable for our actions. What we do in this life matters.

READ 2 CORINTHIANS 5:10-15.

What will all believers be judged on, according to verse 10?

The things we do while in our Bodies

Verse 10 is connected to yesterday's reading concerning what we choose to do while being at home in our earthy bodies. Are we doing what is good or what is bad or worthless? Yes, we will have to give an account for the wrong we've done, but the Lord will also remember our sacrifices, obedience, love, and worship of Him. For the one who has veered off the path, this is an exhortation to repent and get back on track (1 John 1:9). For the weary and persecuted, this is a wealth of encouraging news! The Lord sees and will not forget all the good you are doing in His name (Gal. 6:9).

If we ask forgiveness will we be forgiven

PERSONAL REFLECTION: *How does knowing you will stand before the judgment seat of Christ challenge the wisdom of your decisions and the direction of your goals? How does it encourage you in your walk with Christ?*

In verse 11, Paul states that the fear of the Lord caused them to do something in particular. What was it?

To ~~the~~ fear the Lord.

This is refreshing to me. Do you see what Paul is doing here? He wants the Corinthian church to understand that his ministry to them is born out of love and unselfish motives. Because he has a healthy, reverent fear of the Lord—knowing he will one day stand before Jesus to give an account—he lives openly before them. He has nothing to hide. He's not in ministry to get famous or rich or use the people he serves to prop up his pride.

Each of us is called to ministry in our families, churches, and neighborhoods. As I write these words, I'm motivated to take inventory of the reason I serve others.

PERSONAL REFLECTION: *Ask the Lord to search your heart and reveal any areas where your service or discipleship is selfishly motivated. Write down and confess anything He brings to mind and ask Him to create in you a pure heart.*

I don't feel I am selfishly motivated I really want

On what were some of the Corinthians basing their respect (v. 12)?
- ☒ *Outward Appearance*
- ☐ *The Heart*
- ☐ *Godliness*
- ☒ *Fashion*

Much like in our own day, the worldly Corinthians prized the power and prestige they could lay their eyes on. Paul's suffering, lack of wealth, lack of public speaking skills, and position in society caused many of the Corinthians to discount him. But Paul contended there is something else to consider.

Look up 1 Samuel 16:7. What does the Lord look at and how does this relate to 2 Corinthians 5:12?

The heart He wants us to give Him our heart their

Some of the carnal Corinthians were questioning Paul's sincerity. To answer them, Paul further explains his others-centered ministry in verse 13. He describes two states of mind or behaviors. To whom are each directed?

When Paul seems out of his mind (or religiously fanatical), it's for
God.

When he is clear and soundly instructional, it's for himself.

We're not exactly sure what Paul meant when he used the phrase "out of our mind." It may have meant how people perceived his supernatural experiences, speaking in tongues, or an exceptional emotion toward God. Regardless, what's important is Paul's expression that whether in exceptional or sound behavior, it was all for God and the people he served. Nothing was for selfish gain.

It would be easy for us to perceive Paul's statements as arrogant, if not for verses 14-15.

I mean, how many people can say they're always about the service of God and others? How many can confidently encourage others to look on the secret motivations of their hearts? The answer is no one—apart from Jesus. So let's close with these powerful verses.

Paul said the love of Christ Compels *us (v. 14).*

Different versions of the Bible offer different translations of the Greek word *synechō* (*compels*, NIV), all roughly meaning *to hold together, hold completely, constrain, compress*. It can also mean "to be physically held."[2] Simply put, when the love of Jesus is what's holding and compelling you, you will selflessly bless and serve others. Only then can our motivations be truly selfless.

The next few sentences explain the theology behind this altogether tactile love of Christ.

What did Christ do to show this love, and whom did He do it for?

He died for us.

Write verse 15 below. Then, in your own words, explain how we're to now live based on Jesus' sacrifice for us.

all that those who live should no longer live for themselves But for Him who died for Him who died for them and were raised again And He died for

We're no longer to live for ourselves but for our Savior.

All of 2 Corinthians is a treasure chest filled with the attributes of God, rich theology, wisdom for relationships, comfort, encouragement, along with a host of other jewels. But perhaps no single truth in this letter has the power to so utterly redirect our lives than this one: we're no longer to live for ourselves but for our Savior. We don't want this concept to be what pastor and author Eugene Peterson calls "God talk"—lifeless, Christian terminology that sounds good but never takes root in our hearts. What we need is for this to change us. Our hearts. Actions. Behaviors. Motivations.

I've been thinking a lot about this lately. I realize that sometimes I love the work of Jesus more than I love Jesus. I can get so wrapped up in God's mission, I forget God. A dear leader recently reminded me of how the church at Ephesus had slipped into a similar trap. I revisited Revelation 2:1-4 and I noticed some surprising conditions about this church. Their deeds were good, they worked hard, didn't tolerate evil, were discerning, and persevered through hardship for the Lord's name without weariness. Sounds like some solid performers to me. Yet Jesus rebuked them with sobering words, "I hold this against you," He said, "you have forsaken the love you had at first" (v. 4).

Without the love of Christ compelling us, without our grateful love for Him and His sacrifice, our service will be limp and tired. As my friend reminded me, "Our love for Jesus is everything. He's everything." If we've lost our love for Him, we've lost everything.

As you close today's study, I pray that you sense the love of Jesus constraining you, actually holding you together. As a result of His love may you no longer live for yourself but for the One who gave His life for you. Spend some time in prayer reaffirming your love for Jesus.

Christ Centered Marriage

<u>Christ</u> at the Center of
marriage. Christ is
the centre of Both peoples
heart. Be in it together. 1 Peter 2:30-31

Mens Role   Ladys Role
Let God Lead   Eph 5: 25
Love your wife   Eph 5: 22-24
in the way she   Eph 5: 31-33
will know you want to
love her. Women let him
now you want to follow
him
                Mat 28: 19-20
What is God calling us
to? His love for Church
marriage as a team.
make disciples.

DAY 3
ALL THINGS NEW

2 CORINTHIANS 5:16-21

This past Christmas I surprised my 8-year-old niece, Maryn, with a bearded dragon. He's affectionately known as Oscar Michael Gates, because if our family is going to house a lizard, it at least needs to be a distinguished one. (We may have just discovered that Oscar Michael is in fact a girl. Maryn has decided not to change her name; I don't know what to do about this.) Besides Murphy the beagle, Oscar was Maryn's first pet to have and to hold (and to feed live worms, crickets, and kale) until college do they part. My sister nearly died when I brought it home, but I figured she'd eventually grow accustomed to sheltering a reptile in her home. Seeing that I was flying back to Nashville a couple days later, and bore zero responsibility other than being one fabulous aunt, I was ecstatic about my gift selection.

Since Christmas, my phone has been blowing up with pictures of Maryn feeding Oscar live creatures, bathing him in the sink, stroking him, and toting him all over the house. One night he watched a movie with the family—in my sister and her husband's bed. This makes me so happy. Maryn adores him like I knew she would. I'm starting to wonder if the Christmas Day that Oscar came will be a marker for her—life before and after his arrival.

I can think of a few dividing lines in my life, experiences that marked a before and after. Some were amazing; others painful. We may not consider this on a regular basis, but all of us living today are on the backside of history's most epic event: Christ's death and resurrection. In today's reading— what one scholar quoted as being "one of the most pregnant, difficult, and important in the whole of the Pauline literature"—we'll see how this historic dividing line can do nothing but change our thinking.[3] I wish we were sitting across from one another, because no matter where either of us finds ourselves, I'd like to say to you, and you to me, "Sister, the old has gone, the new has come!"

READ 2 CORINTHIANS 5:16-21.

The phrase *from now on* (*henceforth*, if you're in the King James) indicates a point in time where things will no longer be the same as they were.

How does Paul say that from now on, we will look at people and Jesus differently than before?

Now, look at verse 17. Why will we view Christ and others in a new way?

Remember the Corinthian culture in which Paul was ministering. The people bowed to power, social status, wealth, and prestige. People judged one another according to Hollywood standards. Like we talked about yesterday, the community was judging by outward appearances rather than looking at people's hearts. This past Sunday at church, I spotted an accomplished musician I was anxious to catch up with. At the same time, I caught the eye of someone who's a bit socially awkward with some chronic problems. I didn't rush over to her the way I rushed over to my musician friend. I put on the charm for one but not the other. Simply put, I fell into the trap of regarding someone based on his or her accomplishments, instead of on who each person is in Christ.

PERSONAL TAKE: *Paul said that even he at one time regarded Jesus in purely human terms. What do you think he meant by this?*

Before Paul's conversion, he viewed Jesus through worldly eyes, failing to understand the meaning and significance of Jesus' death and resurrection. Paul most certainly saw Him only as a man, not God's Son. But on the road to Damascus, that all changed.

In verse 17, Paul draws our attention to a dividing line that's already taken place in history. Because of Jesus' incarnation, death, and resurrection, the old order of sin's regime binding us under the law is in the past. All new things have come. We are new creations in Christ. This challenges me at two points of belief in particular: First, how much do I believe Jesus can change me? Second, how much do I believe Jesus can change someone else?

PERSONAL REFLECTION: *Have you given up believing that you or another person could change in a certain area? If so, write about your discouragement and why you lack hope in this area.*

This is hitting me at a personal level. I know so many people right now who've decided that either they can't change or a person close to them can't change. Now I'm not talking about changing from an avid introvert to a people person, or a brunette to a redhead. I don't have in mind a plump chef who's suddenly clearing hurdles as a track star. The old adage that a leopard can't change its spots has some truth to it. But what about the person with the anger or eating problem? Can an addict get free? Is it possible for the father who's a workaholic to have his heart change toward spending time with his children? Can a needy wife find her anchor in God? Might the materially obsessed lay down her credit card for the poor? Yeah, I think all this is absolutely possible and a whole lot more, because remember—from now on—things are different! We no longer view others or ourselves through the frame of our sin and weakness, nor do we puff ourselves up solely on the basis of outward achievement. Things are new. Everything has changed since Jesus Christ came into the world. We now have the very power that raised Christ from the dead working within us (Eph. 1:19-20).

What two words make this change possible? "Therefore if anyone is _____ _____" (2 Cor. 5:17).

Skim back over verses 18-21. Did you pick up on a key word? Write it in the margin.

I have little knack for mathematics, which is why this world has accountants. Praise the Lord for my bookkeeper, Cindy. She doesn't mind hunting down numeric mysteries until the $3.07 espresso receipt is found and any discrepancies between the bank statement and my records are back to the serene number zero. The word for this in accounting is *reconcile*. In other words, what I believe I possess must be checked against what the bank deems I possess. What my record shows doesn't mean anything until Cindy has reconciled it to the bank statement.

Similarly, we can't be put side by side against the goodness and purity of God without our sin being exposed, much like the flaws of an accounting report being exposed when up against the bank statement. In accounting, when my numbers are different from the bank statement, I have to figure out how to get my numbers to agree with the bank—they never seem to want to work the other way. But when it comes to our sinful and broken lives needing to be reconciled to God's perfect standard we discover something altogether astounding here!

Look back at 2 Corinthians 5:18. From whom does reconciliation come? And who gets reconciled to whom?

The word *reconcile* in Scripture means "to change, exchange, change from enmity to friendship, to return to favor with, to reconcile those who are at variance with God."[4] It can also mean "reestablishment of an interrupted or broken relationship."[5] What's so utterly amazing about this is that we don't have to figure out a way to fill the gap or fix the numbers. This is the Lord's work.

While I love a definition, we can understand the word *reconcile* best by seeing how it's used elsewhere in the New Testament. Look up the following references.

Romans 5:10-11. God reconciled us through the death of Jesus when/ while we were _____.

Verse 11 explains that reconciliation is something we:
❏ *receive*   ❏ *hope for*
❏ *earn*   ❏ *already possess*

1 Corinthians 7:10-11. Here Paul is talking about reconciliation between two people. Briefly describe what reconciliation looks like in this situation.

Colossians 1:19-22. List the benefits and blessings that reconciliation through Christ bring us.

2 Corinthians 5:19. What did reconciliation mean God did not do?

I hope you have a clearer and more meaningful picture of the word *reconcile*. As I read these verses along with you, I'm perhaps most thankful for the peace reconciliation brings. You may have noted peace as one of the blessings mentioned in Colossians 1:20, a result of Christ's shed blood for our sin on the cross. Reconciliation always brings peace.

PERSONAL TAKE: *Given what you've learned so far about what it means to be reconciled to God, why is Christ's death for us at the center of reconciliation? In other words, how is Jesus the only One who can make reconciliation with God possible?*

If you've been a Christian for a long time, you may know well the word *reconciliation* and all it means. The trouble is, we can become so accustomed to certain theological terms that we grow tired of them, struggling to drum up new excitement for all they mean. If you find yourself in this place of staleness over the gift of reconciliation, let me propose a thought: You may have only taken this passage halfway down the field.

Look back at 2 Corinthians 5:19-20. How was the message of reconciliation dispersed to the Corinthians?

Just as Paul and his friends shared the message of reconciliation with the Corinthians, it's now our pleasure and task to share it with others. God has chosen us to share His message with the people around us. Paul explicitly says that we are Christ's _____.

PERSONAL REFLECTION: *How does sharing the gospel (God reconciling us to Himself through the sacrifice of Jesus) keep your life as a believer fresh and exciting?*

I visited with a new church plant of about 40 people outside of Milan, Italy. They are all brand new believers, ranging in age from teenagers to a woman named Virginia in her eighties. And my friends, Nina and Michael, have a story for every one of them. My friends are there as ambassadors of Jesus. They're making an appeal in Milan for people to be at peace with God through Christ. This isn't a stale chore for them because it's not a stagnant truth they're circling for the hundredth time. Instead, they're seeing reconciliation take place in all different settings as they tell people the good news. They're seeing people of all ages find peace through Christ, people who were trapped in dead religion or buckling under guilt.

If we simply receive the gift of reconciliation with God and then go about our lives as if it's up to everyone else to figure it out for themselves, we've missed the joy, the adventure, and the point altogether.

Reconciliation always brings peace.

Write verse 21 in the margin and work on memorizing it throughout the rest of the study.

Based on the riches of this verse, why was Paul pleading with the Corinthians to be reconciled to God?

One of my friends honestly shared a few of the things that hold her back from sharing the message: "I think the call to spread this news is really important! But I struggle with being vocal about the gospel. It's something I desire, but I stress out about it so much, worrying that I might be 'that' Christian, that I might offend someone, that I might say something that's not true, that I might be hypocritical. Because of these fears, I often end up saying nothing."

PERSONAL RESPONSE: *What keeps you from sharing the message of reconciliation with others? Lay your reasons and excuses before the Lord and ask Him to make you a passionate minister of reconciliation to the people around you.*

LIVING IN THE TENSION

2 CORINTHIANS 6:1-10

READ 2 CORINTHIANS 5:21–6:2.

I want to begin with the last verse from yesterday's reading because in most translations, the first two verses of chapter 6 are grouped with the last few verses of chapter 5. And we need to read these first two verses in light of the truth from 5:21. In the great exchange, God has extended unfathomable grace, and Paul wanted to make sure the Corinthians didn't receive that grace in vain. The Greek word for *vain* is *kenos* and it means *void, like an empty jug or building, or empty-handed; useless or without effect.*

Last week, I received a bouquet of flowers to cut and separate into jars. Each one offered a fresh scent and dash of cheer to brighten my house. Except I never got around to the cutting and arranging part, and the whole bunch is rotting in murky water in my kitchen. The rubber band is still around the stems. Absurd. This is what it means to receive something in vain. The quality of the gift hasn't changed. The intended purpose is available. But my having it without really receiving it was as good as setting empty jars all over the house. I had the flowers in my possession, but was not making full use of them.

> **PERSONAL REFLECTION:** *You've studied five chapters' worth of information on the church at Corinth. In what ways do you think the Corinthians may have been receiving God's grace in vain?*

In 6:2, we actually get two verses in one because Paul draws from an Old Testament prophecy in Isaiah 49:8. Because this is so important to our understanding of concepts like grace, reconciliation, and salvation, I want you to read Isaiah 49:8-13. Keep in mind this is God's promise to His Servant Jesus, but also relates to the broader deliverance of God's people. This imagery will sweep you up, I promise.

According to verse 9, to whom will Jesus proclaim freedom?

In the margin, write down any other imagery that encourages your heart.

Look at verse 8 and fill in the blanks:

> *In the time of God's favor He will _____.*

> *In the day of salvation He will _____.*

Turn back to 2 Corinthians and consider what Paul is saying. Pulling from the prophet Isaiah's words about how Jesus would bring salvation, Paul is also talking about when.

> *Look at the second half of 2 Corinthians 6:2. When is the time of God's favor (acceptable time), and when is the day of His salvation?*

Do you sense the urgency in Paul's pen? His wrist is pulsing as he writes Isaiah's prophecy, understanding that the prophecy has been fulfilled in Jesus' life, death, and resurrection. It was for the Corinthians, now! It is for us now! The day of God's favor and the day of salvation are right now if you're still breathing. Cut the flowers. Get them in the jars. Don't receive His grace in vain.

The day of God's favor and the day of salvation are right now if you're still breathing.

READ 2 CORINTHIANS 6:3-10.

As we study this letter we must continually keep in mind the criticism Paul was receiving from many of the Corinthians. Misunderstandings and offenses abounded, even though Paul was doing everything he could to minimize them.

> *According to verse 3, what was Paul ultimately trying to protect?*

Paul had been known to throw down some lists in his writings, whether it was the fruit of the spirit or vices to flee. In your reading today, he listed a slew of trials he'd been through along with some virtues he displayed in those sufferings, thanks be to the Spirit. The challenging thing about lists is truly reading them, as opposed to just scanning them or checking certain items off them. I want you to resist the quick glance and encourage you to consider each description as an experience Paul actually walked through, maybe one you too have tread.

REVIEW 2 CORINTHIANS 6:4B-5:

Circle the general descriptions below and square the specific ones:

troubles	hardships	distresses
riots	imprisonments	hard work
sleepless nights	hunger	beatings

REVIEW 2 CORINTHIANS 6:6-7B:

Keeping in mind all that Paul has suffered, write the four virtues that characterized his life in the left-hand column. Include the preposition in front of each description (v. 6a).

1.   1.

2.   2.

3.   3.

4.   4.

We can be tempted to look at these four virtues Paul displayed during his trials, lump them together in a hurry, then conclude that Paul was one great guy. But let's look at these more closely to get at the heart of this list.

Purity in this case is the opposite of corruption. It can also mean simplicity of heart or sincerity. Paul didn't have anything up his sleeve. His motives were pure before God and the Corinthians. He wanted what was best for them without a secret or selfish agenda.

Knowledge (or understanding) is knowing someone in a personal way. I love how one scholar put it, "This is not 'knowledge-as-instrument' but 'knowledge' as a *person shaper*" (emphasis mine).[6] Paul had a relationship with the Corinthians that was intuitive and personal.

Patience is the translation of the Greek word *makroythmia*. It's a people-oriented patience. It can mean slowness in avenging wrongs, biting your tongue when wounded, or remaining calm while awaiting an outcome. It also means long-suffering and enduring with people who can be difficult to love or slow to change.

Kindness can mean moral goodness in action. While patience is reactive, kindness is proactive. It can mean being helpful, beneficial to others, generous.

> **PERSONAL REFLECTION:** *While I believe all the virtues of Christ are interconnected, which one of these four comes most naturally for you and which one do you struggle with the most? Explain.*

This morning I confessed to the Lord the lack of some of these virtues in my life while dealing with some difficult situations. Let me put it this way: I find demonstrating purity, understanding, patience, and kindness an absolute breeze toward the people I like. It's all those other people that cause these virtues to get jammed up. The critics Paul was writing to were those other people, and still he responded in Christlikeness. But how? We need to fill in the right hand column to find out.

In the right hand column, write four means or methods Paul used (vv. 6b-7). (Interesting note: In the Greek, the first four descriptions in the list are one word; the second four are two words. This may mean Paul was setting them apart, perhaps the first four being the manner in which these qualities were displayed; the second being the means.[7])

When people sin against us or someone we love, when they're critical or emotionally unavailable, when they betray or unfairly accuse, we need something far more than a mere list of virtues to emulate. We need to respond in the Holy Spirit, in sincere love, in truthful speech, and in the power of God.

I know many of you are in profoundly difficult situations. People close to you are pushing the limits of your capacity for goodness. The stress of an interminable trial has left you without reserve. You're just trying to keep everyone in the house alive, forget about adding virtues into the mix. This is when what we discovered in the right-hand column becomes essential. The reality is neither Paul, nor we, can come by purity, knowledge, patience, and kindness without supernatural help.

HOLY SPIRIT: *What other name is given for the Holy Spirit in John 14:26?*

SINCERE LOVE: *Look back at 2 Corinthians 5:14. Whose love drives Paul?*

According to Romans 5:5, where does true, selfless love come from?

TRUTHFUL SPEECH: *Paul may well be referring to the proclamation of the gospel. Look at Romans 1:16. What does the gospel carry with it?*

POWER OF GOD: *Read Ephesians 1:18-19. To whom does God give His great power?*

What weapons does Paul carry in his left and right hands (2 Cor. 6:7)?
- ❏ *shrewd wit*
- ❏ *gregarious personality*
- ❏ *savvy speech*
- ❏ *righteousness*

When we look at biblical themes such as sacrificial love, turning the other cheek, and displaying virtues to difficult people, we can mistakenly conjure images of weak and doormat-ish, needy people. We need to remember that righteousness is anything but weak and can be used as a weapon for good. Oh, yes, it is humble and kind and long-suffering, but the righteousness of Christ is also strong and capable of repelling evil. (You can meditate on this further in Ephesians 6:11-13.) The point being, sometimes in our painful and difficult relationships, we need to get in there with some spiritual weapons and fight.

We need to remember that righteousness is anything but weak and can be used as a weapon for good.

READ 2 CORINTHIANS 6:8-10.

PERSONAL REFLECTION: *Look through the following list of couplets and circle the ones you relate to the most. Describe how both sides of the coin have been simultaneously true, mostly focusing on the positive side of the couplet. (Matthew 5:1-12 is another passage for further consideration.)*

As deceivers (imposters), yet true

As unknown, yet recognized

As dying, and look—we live

As being disciplined, yet not killed

As grieving, yet always rejoicing

As poor, yet enriching many

As having nothing, yet possessing everything

How can we have nothing yet everything? Be unknown yet recognizable? Poor yet making many rich? These are supernatural realities that are only possible for believers. I think of George Müller who came from Germany to England, poor as a pauper, and opened up an orphanage for thousands of homeless children. Or the Englishman Hudson Taylor who was called to minister to China, at times slept in pig's pens, yet he journaled about the fullness of Christ bursting in his heart.

These are the mysteries that characterize the life of a believer. That we can be empty with something still to give, sad while tapping into a reservoir of joy, invisible to others but keenly seen by God. Living these dichotomies, while difficult, can be particularly sweet. Because we know that whatever good grows amidst the rocky soil can only be a miracle from Him.

DAY 5
UNEQUALLY YOKED

2 CORINTHIANS 6:11–7:1

If parsing some of yesterday's verses was a bit tedious, today's reading begins with a straightforward plea for earnest relationship. Take a moment to quiet your heart before the Lord asking Him to reveal His Word to you today.

READ 2 CORINTHIANS 6:11-13.

PERSONAL REFLECTION: *Have you ever opened your heart wide to someone only to have that person close his or her heart toward you? Describe what this felt like in as much detail as you can.*

Speaking freely, opening our hearts wide, and not withholding our affections, seems like a recipe for pain. If I allow myself to be this vulnerable in a relationship, I throw open a window that someone I love could slam down on my fingers. Isn't it safer to protect and batten down our hearts to the winds of rejection and betrayal? Safer, maybe. But this isn't the way of love. Or fullness of life. Or authentic community.

Make no mistake, Paul was begging for a two-way street in relationship, but he couldn't force it into being. He was pleading for return affection from the Corinthians, but he couldn't control the outcome. Despite these realities, Paul's commitment to them wasn't deterred nor was his love for them weakened.

PERSONAL RESPONSE: *Is there anyone you're withholding affection from because you're afraid of being hurt? If you're willing to entrust the person's response (or lack thereof) to the Lord, write a prayer asking for the Lord to give you unbridled kind speech, a wide-stretched heart, and abundant affection for this person—no matter his or her response.*

The next section can seem abrupt. But if we keep in mind Paul's desire for unadulterated affection, I think the following verses fit snugly.

READ 2 CORINTHIANS 6:14–7:1.

We can pretty much divide humanity into two segments: those who grew up in the church being taught about what it means to be "unequally yoked" and those who didn't. If you're part of the first group you're probably remembering youth group summer camps where this passage was used to drive home one point and one point only: don't date non-Christians. If you're in the second group, you're wondering if this is a new way to do eggs. (That was my poor attempt at lightening things up—it's the last homework day of the week and you've earned it.)

Let's begin by defining the term *yoke* so we're all on the same page (your version may say "mismatched"). *Yoke*: "a wooden bar or frame by which two draft animals (as oxen) are joined at the heads or necks for working together."[8] In Deuteronomy 22:10, the law prohibited a person to plow with a calf and a donkey together, as the calf was considered clean and the donkey unclean. Also, these mismatched animals would pull the yoke in differing ways and with differing force.

PERSONAL TAKE: *Based on this illustration, why do you think having a binding, intimate relationship with an unbeliever is incompatible? Take some time with this.*

> Do not be yoked together with unbelievers. For what do righteousness and wickedness have in common? Or what fellowship can light have with darkness? What harmony is there between Christ and Belial? Or what does a believer have in common with an unbeliever? What agreement is there between the temple of God and idols?
>
> 2 Corinthians 6:14-16a

Look at the comparisons in the margin and fill in the missing blanks from verses 14-16. (I've given you the NIV translation for continuity, but feel free to use the words in your own translation.)

What do righteousness and wickedness have in _____?

What_____ can light have with darkness?

What _____ is there between Christ and Belial?

What does a believer and unbeliever have in _____?

What _____ is there between the temple of God and idols?

PERSONAL TAKE: *While Paul is not explicit about the types of relationships this applies to, what types do you think he has in mind here? (I think it's more than one.)*

If you're attached to someone in a double harness and your passions differ, world views clash, values aren't in sync, and destinations are in different locations, how in the world is this going to work? On the other hand, we've seen Paul clearly preaching reconciliation to a lost world, so he certainly doesn't mean we shouldn't have relationships with unbelievers. Let's keep going. I think things will become clearer.

Read Acts 17:24. Where does God no longer dwell?

Back to 2 Corinthians 6:16, Paul says that we are the temple of the living God. This verse has major implications for our relationships. What are they?

Paul quotes several Old Testament passages here, weaving them together into a call for holiness. In verse 17, Paul quotes from the prophet Isaiah, who at the time was proclaiming freedom for the Israelites from the pagan city of Babylon.

READ ABOUT GOD'S DELIVERANCE OF HIS PEOPLE IN ISAIAH 52:9-11.

Describe the excitement and hope of the setting.

PERSONAL REFLECTION: *When it comes to your being separate from what the world desires and prizes, do you look at the prospect as a burden or a joy? Explain.*

Summarizing this string of Old Testament references, Paul reminds us of Israel's history that has flowed into our present. God no longer dwells in temples made by hands but in our hearts! He lives among us, and we're His people.

As a result of these promises, what are we urged to do in 2 Corinthians 7:1?

According to 1 John 1:9, what is one way we purify ourselves?

The verses from 2 Corinthians 6:11–7:1, are often framed in a way that highlights the negative: don't be unequally yoked, don't touch anything unclean, don't get contaminated by all that sin out there, come out (from all the fun). While some clear "negatives" are present, actually the context is for an entirely positive purpose. We can't miss the love and relationship here!

> *Look back at 2 Corinthians 6:18. What will God be to us and what will we be to Him?*

We are the sons and daughters of God (an interesting addition Paul made to the text from 2 Samuel 7:14), and He is a father to us. God yearns to dwell with us right here in the middle of our earthly lives, walk beside us in our comings and goings, tend us as a loving Father tends His beloved daughters. Do you see how this changes everything about how we view the concept of being unequally yoked? Suddenly we're not talking about staying separate from the world because Christians can never have fun (Sometimes the team motto feels like it's the word *no*.). Instead, this is a plea to separate ourselves from anything that might hinder our knowing and being known in Christ. It's for the sake of our freedom. In holiness we've been set apart for an unrivaled privilege and adventure, unfettered. Do we really want to risk that honor by contaminating our bodies and spirits and letting our lusts rule the day? Do we want to compromise the freedom of our relationship with Christ by being deeply bound to someone who is not a believer?

In holiness we've been set apart for an unrivaled privilege and adventure, unfettered.

Your gut answer in this moment may be a swirl of yeses and noes. I surely understand this. If you've ever desired a consequential relationship with someone who doesn't share your faith in Jesus, this can be a painful prospect. We've all longed for what this world has to offer while resisting the real life Jesus longs to give us. However, there is simply no unclean thing worth touching at the expense of holding the blessings the Father longs to give you. No deep and binding relationship with an unbeliever is worth forfeiting unveiled intimacy with Jesus. No life in the foreign city of Babylon can touch the trove of adventure that accompanies a clean heart in which God dwells. No title or position rivals the title of Daughter of the Lord Almighty.

PERSONAL RESPONSE: *Respond to one of the three below:*

> *1. If you're already bound to someone through marriage or a contract who's not a believer, please know the Lord's grace abounds. Ask God to bring the other party into a relationship with Himself. Pray for grace to be a bold and loving witness for Him (1 Cor. 7:12-14).*

> *2. If you're currently in a situation where you're unequally yoked and you're able to untie that knot, put this before the Lord. Ask for His courage and strength to follow Him in obedience. (This doesn't apply if you're married.)*

3. If you're considering entering into a binding relationship you know isn't from the Lord, what steps do you need to take to keep from tying yourself to that person?

You've accomplished so much this week. You've considered what it means to be truly home, whether on earth or in heaven. You've thought about the emphasis you put on your temporal body and how one day that body will be swallowed up with an incorruptible one. You've been reminded that how you live on this earth matters, what it means to be reconciled to God, and what it means to be a minister of that reconciliation to a weary world that so longs for it. The mysteries of suffering and simultaneously possessing joy are truths you've mined. You've also been encouraged to stretch your hearts open just a little wider even if what you most want to do is self-protect; love does not withhold. And finally, you've been refreshed by the loving heart behind God's command for us not to be unequally yoked with unbelievers. A Father and His protective love for His daughter is what lay at the heart of this plea.

Come out, dear one. Come out. The new has come.

SESSION 4 VIEWER GUIDE

THE NEW HAS COME

GROUP DISCUSSION:

Kelly said, "We don't want to be tied to another person in such a way where their direction in life holds power over God's calling in our life." What does that mean?

In light of the first question, why is being in a close relationship with an unbeliever so costly?

Do a quick evaluation—is your lifestyle and the things you value markedly different than what's important in our current culture? Explain.

Why can we not bear both the sacred and the sacrilegious at the same time? How do we attempt to? What are the consequences?

Usually we have seen the command to not be unequally yoked in a negative light, but in reality, it is very positive. In what way?

What does God being a Father to you mean to you?

What one thing stood out to you from this video?

The music featured in this session is from Kelly's Hymns & Hallelujahs *CD. Video sessions and the CD are available for purchase at* **LIFEWAY.COM/ALLTHINGSNEW**

Hummingbird Cake (serves 12)

INGREDIENTS:

CAKE: ½ - 3/4 cup pecans

1 package plain yellow cake mix

1 (8-oz) can crushed pineapple with juice, undrained

1 cup mashed bananas

½ cup vegetable or canola oil

½ cup water

3 eggs

1 teaspoon vanilla extract

1 teaspoon cinnamon

FROSTING: I package (8 oz) cream cheese, softened

½ stick butter, softened

3 ½ cups powdered sugar, sifted

2 tablespoon vanilla

My mom made this for me on my last birthday. Yes, my mom still makes me birthday cakes if she happens to be in town, because you never outgrow a birthday cake from your mom. I later found out that this is a traditional south-ern cake with bananas and pineapple. You need fairly ripe bananas for sure, so if your bananas are too ripe to do something healthy with them, consider this cake.

DIRECTIONS

For the cake: Preheat oven to 350 degrees. Spread whole pecans on a dry baking sheet and toast a few minutes to add deep flavor. Shake pan once during cooking to toss, and watch closely so they do not burn. Chop pe-cans once they have cooled a bit.

Combine the cake mix, crushed pineapple with juice, mashed bananas, oil, water, eggs, vanilla, and cinnamon in a large bowl with an electric mixer about 2 minutes until smooth. Pour into a greased 13x9x2-inch pan. Bake for approximately 35 minutes, or until an inserted toothpick comes out clean. Cool completely before frosting.

NOTE: You may also use two round pans. Adjust baking time as needed, typically 30-35 minutes.

For the frosting: Beat the cream cheese and butter with mixer until smooth, and slowly add the powdered sugar. Then add vanilla and beat until fluffy. Frost cake and sprinkle the toasted pecans on top. Cover and refrigerate until ready to serve.

SESSION 5

THE GRACE
OF GIVING

My 5-year-old nephew, Will, and my 3-year-old niece, Harper, were in my possession for the day. My brother had dropped them off at eight in the morning and was picking them up after work at five o'clock—I was tired by approximately 9:42 a.m. This is simply due to the fact that I'm not used to fielding a million questions before breakfast. Which brings me to breakfast. It's shocking the energy necessary for toasting blueberry waffles, cutting them into non-chokable sized pieces, dousing them with enough syrup to be visible to the toddler's eye while accounting for absorption—because once it soaks in, they don't buy that it's actually there. There's a science to all this.

This is not to mention the remarkable brain power needed for choosing the appropriately colored cups for the right child. I've learned that yellow, pink, green, and blue cups can be interchanged at your whim until the day they catch onto color, at which point your life is officially over. The who-gets-what-colored-cup conversation is a universal one that cannot be solved by simply assigning each child his or her favorite color. Why? Because the favorite colors change without notice. We adults do not have the expertise to crack this code. It's a dynamic, complex formula that only children know and can torture us with.

I hustled Will off to school and before I knew it, the time came for Harper and me to return and pick him up. Time flies when the kids are gone. Will had no sooner nestled into his car seat when he pulled three Chinese coins out of his pocket, coins his teacher had given him. They were colorful, sparkly little things—otherwise known as kindling logs for the argument that was about to catch fire in the backseat of the car. Will flashing his coins around was perfectly torturous for Harper, who isn't in school yet, thus isn't taking home money. I tried to downplay the whole thing. "Harps, this is fake money," I explained. "You can't buy anything with those silly coins." This did little to deter her as Will clinked the coins, inspected them, tilted them so as to reflect and refract the rays of sun bearing through the car window. One of them was even pink—if Will didn't give Harper one of those coins she was going to sever her car seat harness with her bare teeth and rip them out of his stubby little fingers.

When you're trying to keep a moving vehicle on the road, it's difficult to get into philosophical discussions with preschoolers about sharing. The concept of enjoying something that is yours while

simultaneously realizing that it's only yours because it's been given to you, or because you were graced with the power to earn it, or because you were born into the optimal circumstances to receive it, therefore arriving at the conclusion that your reasonable act of service is to share your fake coins (and your real ones), is a difficult concept whether you're 4 or 40.

What are we doing with the gifts God has given us? How are we using our resources for His Kingdom?

We know inherently as believers that everything we have has been given to us by the Lord. Our homes, cars, 401(k)s, jobs, second homes, savings, health, clothes, food, furniture, spending cash, the chairs we sit on, the beds we curl up in, and the kitchen tables we dine around all come from Him. Every possession is a gift. We may have worked hard for it, but it's still a gift because God gives us the opportunity and power to work. We may have made a smart investment— but it's still a gift because God gives us the wisdom and wit to grow our money or turn that business around or choose the right stock. So, the question is, what are we doing with the gifts God has given us? How are we using our resources for His Kingdom?

Are we making everlasting deposits by spending ourselves to nourish hungry bodies, mend aching hearts, and propel the gospel to the ends of the earth with the blessings God has given us?

Out of the 13 chapters Paul writes to the Corinthians, two of them are about the grace, joy, and privilege of generosity. I use these three words purposefully because these are the words Paul uses. And they are so different from the words we normally think of when it comes to giving—words like sacrifice, duty, and misery. Later this week and at the top of the next, we'll study an actual scenario that involves a poor Gentile church in Macedonia, a poor Jewish church in Jerusalem, and the

rather affluent church in Corinth we've come to know.

I won't give away the details but what I want you to notice is the excitement that comes when we choose obedience through generosity. When we sacrificially give for Kingdom purposes we get to know the heart of God, we more deeply attach to the people we're called to care for, we move out into deeper waters of faith and grace, and we share in the privilege of being part of something far more compelling than what money can buy. We'll notice Paul and Titus (and God Himself—2 Cor. 8:16) bursting with excitement over the financial blessing they can't wait for the Jerusalem church to receive. But with equal zeal, they can't wait for the blessing the Corinthian church will receive as a result of being the ones to supply that blessing.

Fly forward nearly two thousand years and God's heart is still beating for the poor, the lost, the wounded, the orphan, and the widow. He's still desperate for us to step out in faith and give beyond what we think we can because we've been given a grace to do so. Because it's a privilege to be a participant in His work. Because it's where the joy is. Because everything we have has been given to us.

On the way home from Will's preschool that afternoon, I witnessed the sprouting seeds of what God was already cultivating in his heart. "Here you go, Harper," he said while handing her the coin with a smile. "You can have it." Harper was happy, Will still had two coins, and all the way home there was joy.

DAY 1
WISDOM FOR RELATIONSHIPS

2 CORINTHIANS 7:2-10

In case you've lost track, you've completed three weeks of homework and journeyed through six chapters and one verse of 2 Corinthians. Do you know what this means? It means you can absolutely finish! You've maybe sacrificed a bit of sleep or a few television shows to get here. You've laid aside a luxury or changed a routine to make this happen. What I know is that you've made this happen. You've planned for it and protected it. And don't get down on yourself if every blank is not filled in or every answer circled—we're showing up for intimacy with Jesus and life-change, not good grades.

Just the fact that you're still here shows both desire and discipline. My personal times in Scripture have been characterized by both, sometimes desire more than discipline or the other way around. When desire is lacking, it's sheer discipline that gets me through. Some may consider this pure legalism, that if my heart's not in it I might as well just stay under the covers or get to work early. But I don't think this is true. Plenty of days I don't feel like exercising or eating right or being friendly—or flossing—but discipline fills in the gaps. And what I've found about sticking with a Bible study and being committed to a weekly gathering is that oftentimes discipline ends up leading to desire. While a sense of duty may initiate my study, somewhere in the process a change takes place and duty becomes delight. So keep at it. If discipline hasn't quite turned into desire, just give it a little more time. And for goodness' sake, pray for it. The Lord loves to give this to us.

READ 2 CORINTHIANS 7:2-4.

In case you'd forgotten how desperately Paul longs for a restored relationship with the church at Corinth, he's still on that bandwagon in today's passage. You may have thought all this pleading and longing had wrapped up with chapter 6, but surprise—he's got more love. How is it even possible?

PERSONAL REFLECTION: *How has Paul's persistence and committed attitude toward the Corinthians encouraged you to keep at a difficult relationship? Be specific. (Look back at 2 Cor. 5:14 to remind yourself where this love finds its origin.)*

True or False: In verses 2-3, Paul cites that he hadn't wronged, corrupted, or exploited anyone so he could throw the hammer down on the Corinthians.

PERSONAL RESPONSE: *One writer translated Paul's words in verse 3 as, "You are in my very heart, and you will be there in death and life alike."[1] Who has a place in your heart like no other? With whom would you live and die? Take some time to pray for these precious relationships—even if they're strained right now.*

What two things does Paul say he has in the Corinthians (v. 4a)?

Biblically speaking, pride isn't normally a positive attribute, but in this case we get to go for it! We do well to take pride in another person who's growing in Christ. It's good to show our confidence in those we've poured into. I take pride in the girls I disciple when I see them making decisions that please the Lord. I have a ton of confidence in my parents who have had a faithful run of ministry. I'm overjoyed when I see my young nieces and nephews tottering out on faith. While I may celebrate these things in my heart, I want to be better at actually expressing my enthusiasm for the people around me.

Sometime in the next seven days write a note of encouragement to someone you take pride in. Open your heart wide to him/her.

> *"Often a wise leader knows how to blend words of confrontation with words of encouragement."*
>
> *- George Guthrie[2]*

I appreciate Paul's wisdom here. He boosts the Corinthians in all the ways he genuinely can be proud of them, meanwhile not shirking from the areas that needed addressing. I love what George Guthrie said about this: "Often a wise leader knows how to blend words of confrontation with words of encouragement."[2]

You may be wondering why Paul is suddenly talking about his pride in the Corinthians, his confidence in them, and the encouragement he has because of them. Not for nothing but they've been a little disappointing. They've bought into the false teachers, accused Paul of being a fraud, cozied up a little too much with the unbelievers in Corinth. So what's going on here? Why Paul's seemingly sudden change of attitude? Part of it has to do with the way he laid out his letter. Let me show you what I mean.

Remember that earlier in our study Paul explained why he had to change his travel plans to visit the Corinthians. In the middle of that explanation, he took an approximate five chapter hiatus to discuss the nature of true Christian ministry (2:14–7:4). The Corinthians had been looking for someone with worldly credentials such as wealth, notoriety, and status with the upper echelon. Paul responded that his was a humble ministry all about hearts, led by the Spirit, housed in fragile vessels. His ministry was not about himself but all about Jesus, focused on eternity instead of the temporal, grounded in reconciliation, and often characterized by suffering.

PERSONAL REFLECTION: *What part of Paul's description of Christian ministry has been the biggest revelation to you? Explain.*

Paul now picks back up with the good news of a reunion with Titus and the Corinthians' renewed love and commitment to him.

For the sake of continuity, read 2 Corinthians 2:12-13, then move to 2 Corinthians 7:5-7. How did God bring comfort to Paul?

There is no comfort quite like the comfort of God that comes through a friend. In Paul's case it was the comfort of God, through the Corinthians, then through Titus—the comfort train chugging from Corinth to Macedonia. If we were handing out Oscars for *2 Corinthians,* the movie, Titus would win "Best Male Supporting Actor" hands down. Since he's about to make several more appearances, let's do some quick research on him.

Read Galatians 2:1-3. What nationality was Titus and what did he choose not to do while in Jerusalem?

Read Titus 1:4. Keeping in mind that Paul was a circumcised Jew, how does he refer to Titus?

This may not seem like a big deal today, but the fact that Titus was an uncircumcised Greek and one of Paul's spiritual sons is a transformational demonstration of the gospel. Circumcised Jews wouldn't have had anything to do with uncircumcised Gentiles pre-Christ. But when Jesus came, He tore down the dividing wall between Jews and Gentiles (Eph. 2:11-22), offering salvation to all nations, tribes, and tongues (Col. 3:11). Paul, a Jew of all Jews, could now consider Titus not only a dear partner in ministry, but also his very son. This is one of example of how, through Christ's work, the old has gone and the new has come (2 Cor. 5:17).

READ 2 CORINTHIANS 7:7.

List everything the Corinthians expressed to Titus about Paul. What did this bring about in Paul?

CONTINUE READING 2 CORINTHIANS 7:8-10.

The letter Paul is referring to is the one we read about in 2 Corinthians 2:4. Remember Paul had decided to write the Corinthians a letter instead of making another painful visit to them. Sometimes, conflict needs to be resolved in person; other times the situation is so raw that sending a message is the wisest move. Biblical examples support both. And sometimes, there's just no way to know what's right, apart from the leading of the Holy Spirit.

PERSONAL TAKE: *Explain why Paul didn't regret that his letter had caused the church sorrow (vv. 8-9).*

It's true that Paul didn't regret the sorrowful letter he wrote to the Corinthians by the time we reach this point in the epistle. But remember that earlier in Paul's letter he was greatly pained over having to confront them and what the confrontation might do to their relationship (2 Cor. 2:1-4). Addressing sensitive and difficult issues with people we care for is never a pleasant task, but it can rescue a person from destruction in the end. As my friend Jessica pointed out, "True godly love cares more for the sanctification of a loved one than being popular to them."

Our godly decisions don't always lead to tidy emotions.

Much like Paul's conflicting feelings in verse 8, our godly decisions don't always lead to tidy emotions. In one sense, Paul had no remorse over the painful letter because he now knew it had helped the Corinthians. But in the agonizing in-between stages, he'd experienced some measure of regret. The reason Paul could release this regret was because the sorrow caused by the letter led to the church's repentance. This word *repentance* literally means to change your mind or to turn around.

Godly sorrow leads to _____

Worldly sorrow leads to _____

PERSONAL TAKE: *Think of a time when you were sorry about something only because of what it cost you: exposure, shame, loss of relationship, or freedom. Would you consider this worldly sorrow or godly sorrow?*

Now consider a time when your sorrow over your sin led you to seek God's forgiveness and change your ways. Is this wordly sorrow or godly sorrow?

Briefly explain the difference between the two.

Godly sorrow leads us to repentance, but so does something else. What is it according to Romans 2:4?

A friend of mine pointed out that not only does godly sorrow lead to repentance, but it also leads to intimacy. When we're truly sorry for our sin, we return to a walk of obedience to Christ, and a new level of intimacy is established. Take heart if you're experiencing the grief of godly sorrow, for this train's only destination is repentance. Then, once you reach repentance, you'll continue onto restoration. Somewhere along the way, as you gaze out the window, you'll realize your bags of regret never got on.

THE GOOD OF GODLY SORROW

2 CORINTHIANS 7:11-16

Have you ever been alarmed at how little you know your own self?

Why did I respond like that? From where did this inclement weather of emotions come sweeping in? What's this ambivalence I'm feeling?

It's a strange phenomenon that our familiar selves can occasionally feel like folks we've never met. Sometimes we need a rocky path to jostle the confusion free or a godly sorrow to expose our true hearts. I wish there were an easier way to reach the genuine marrow of our beings, but the encouraging news from today's text is that godly sorrow not only exposes who we really are, it actually produces change. Results. A difference. Like, we're not who we used to be. When we experience the sorrow God intends (2 Cor. 7:9), the dross and impurities fall away, and we emerge anew. I think you're going to love today's word.

When we experience the sorrow God intends, the dross and impurities fall away and we emerge anew.

READ 2 CORINTHIANS 7:11-12.

List the seven results godly sorrow produced in the Corinthians. (I filled in the first one for you.)

1. *Earnestness or Diligence*

2.

3.

4.

5.

6.

7.

The painful letter Paul had written to the Corinthians had been received in the best possible way. They didn't fight back, become defensive, spread gossip, or chuck the faith. They'd messed up, but Paul's point wasn't to focus on their wrongs; instead, he longed for them to respond and be restored. And they'd done both.

Let's look more intently at each of their positive responses.

1. The Corinthians were stirred out of passivity and complacency, **BECOMING EARNEST** and diligent in what really mattered.

2. The desire they had to **CLEAR THEMSELVES** doesn't mean they hadn't done anything wrong. Instead, it was an eager desire to explain their actions, admitting guilt where needed.

3. The **INDIGNATION** they expressed could be anger at the person who sinned mentioned in chapter 2, the false prophets who had been slandering Paul, or even themselves for being complacent while all this was going on.

4. They had a newly awakened **ALARM/FEAR**. This word can mean awe-inspired reverence for God or a sobering respect in relation to a person, perhaps Paul.

5. The deep **LONGING OR DESIRE** was an "intense positive interest in something. Marked by a sense of dedication."[3] The church at Corinth had a renewed longing for Paul and his friends.

6. They also had a special **CONCERN/ZEAL/ENTHUSIASM** for Paul and the things of the Lord.

7. And lastly, all this had led to **JUSTICE**. Some translations use the words *vindication* or *punishment*, but in this list of all positive and heart-warming descriptions, justice seems best. Specifically, this could relate to the punishment of the offender (2 Cor. 2:5-11) or generally, a commitment to deal with sin correctly and lovingly.

> **PERSONAL REFLECTION:** *Review the previous list. Which of the seven have you experienced as a result of the Lord taking you through a season of godly sorrow? In other words, how has your repentance led you to similar responses?*

For me, the most significant season of repentance in my life led to a deeper desire to esteem obedience in a culture that blurs right and wrong. Black got blacker, and white got whiter. I became more concerned about holiness in my life and in the lives of those I serve. The words Paul used in verse 11 are words of passion and feeling—there's not a bland description in the bunch. I believe the more repentant we are, the more passionate we become for righteousness and goodness.

According to verse 11, what had the Corinthians shown or proven themselves to be?

Once you were alienated and hostile in your minds because of your evil actions. But now He has reconciled you by His physical body through His death, to present you holy, faultless, and blameless before Him.
Colossians 1:21-22, HCSB

The Corinthians were innocent, pure, clear. Yes, they had sinned but they had made things right through repentance, thus they could be called clean. This is such a testament to how God takes the shame and guilt and record of our past and restores us to innocence.

READ COLOSSIANS 1:21-22.

What makes us pure and blameless?

In today's opener I mentioned how godly sorrow can lead us through the confusion we sometimes feel in our hearts to a place of clarity. In keeping with this idea, review 2 Corinthians 7:12 and write the purpose Paul gave for writing the painful letter.

Remember that the LORD your God led you on the entire journey these 40 years in the wilderness, so that He might humble you and test you to know what was in your heart, whether or not you would keep His commands.
Deuteronomy 8:2, HCSB

The Corinthians' hearts had been revealed and their motives disclosed. They'd aligned themselves with truth and wanted to act in accordance with that truth. But the path to get there hadn't been easy for either side. Paul had been misunderstood and wounded, and we can be sure a ton of feelings had been battered. The Corinthians didn't understand why Paul had seemingly stood them up. I can only imagine the gossip grapevine spreading through town, false teachers luring people away in the church's hour of weakness, and people taking sides down the middle of the sanctuary. Thankfully, Titus had stepped in as the messenger and peacemaker. How this was resolved is church work at its best.

Read Deuteronomy 8:2 in the margin. Why did God allow the Israelites to endure the wilderness? How is this similar to what came from the Corinthians' experience?

LET'S CLOSE OUR DAY BY RETURNING TO 2 CORINTHIANS 7:13-16.

Try to picture the day Titus came to Macedonia and found Paul, the two of them reunited for the first time in months. Imagine Paul's anxiety having reached its crest after wondering and agonizing over how his beloved church in Corinth had responded to the painful but needed corrective letter. Did they hate him? Had the church blown up? Had God's work in Corinth been lost? Then, envision Titus, after having embraced Paul, saying, "It's all good, Paul. It's so, so good. They're doing great! They understand they've messed up, and they're really sorry. And not just sorry for being caught, but truly sorry before the Lord. They heard you, and they've made changes. Heart changes. Oh, and they're dying to see you, Paul—they're just dying to see you!"

PERSONAL RESPONSE: *Not all conflicts work out like this. However, I believe a great many more can be resolved if we lovingly confront the situation in the way Paul did. Is there any relationship you need to fight for like Paul and Titus fought for their relationship with the Corinthians? Spend some time praying, journaling, or reflecting with the Lord about this.*

Christian relationships are not easy, but they're worth it. We're simply not meant to tread through life alone without someone to douse our souls with refreshment, without a bunch of fellow sojourners to brag about because we're just so proud of their obedience to the Lord. We're not meant to exist without this band known as the church, and in this church, we're doubly blessed if we find ourselves a Titus or two. These are the ones we achingly miss when they're absent (2 Cor. 2:13). They're the ones who tell us the truth and expect truth from us, partly because they already know it. They stand in the gap for us and help shoulder the unpleasant tasks. They're willing to do the hard stuff because they love us, and they love the body of Christ.

Christian relationships are not easy, but they're worth it.

PERSONAL RESPONSE: *Close today by thanking God for the dear friends He's given you. Pray you can be a Titus to them and they to you.*

DAY 3
THE PRIVILEGE OF GENEROSITY

2 CORINTHIANS 8:1-9

I'm so excited to explore chapters 8–9 with you over the next few days. Things are about to get really practical, especially in an area of our Christian lives where we often struggle to give God control. Call it your purse, wallet, or leather bag—He wants in. Actually He wants us to dig in there ourselves and cheerfully—and I do mean with some serious happiness—offer Him our resources, in particular for those in need. Before you start reading today's text, ask the Lord to open your mind to receive and apply whatever He reveals to you in the next few days.

But first, here's some background for today's reading. The Macedonian churches mentioned in this chapter included the churches at Philippi, Thessalonica, and Berea. These churches were extremely poor and in the middle of a significant trial. Still, they were eager to give to the Jewish believers who were also living in extreme poverty.

READ 2 CORINTHIANS 8:1-9.

What two seemingly opposite things resulted in rich generosity (v. 2)?

PERSONAL TAKE: *How do you think it's possible for seemingly opposites like joy and extreme poverty to overflow into generosity? (Note: generosity isn't necessarily linked to having a lot of money.)*

Occasionally when reading the Bible, a single word will jump out at me. One word in the middle of sentences, narrative, punctuations, and theological truths will wave its arms and say, *look at me, Kel*. This happened when I reached 2 Corinthians 8:4. It's the word *privilege*. Other translations may use the word *favor*, but regardless, the sentiment is the same. The Greek word is a beautiful one, *charis*. It can mean *grace, benefit, favor,* or *delight*. This deeply impoverished Macedonian church, made up of Gentiles, had a deep desire to give to the Jewish believers in Jerusalem. They didn't look at giving as a chore, duty, or hardship; rather they saw it as a privilege! As if they had the inside scoop on a special deal that meant giving even more away to their Jewish brothers and sisters.

PERSONAL REFLECTION: *Put a mark on the spectrum below that represents how you look at monetary giving.*

Avoid   *Eager*

|--|

Some of us want to hold onto our money because we love to save and invest. This is me. I don't want to be caught unprepared, so I like being able to turn some money into more money by putting it in places where it can grow. When I first learned the meaning of compounding interest, I thought it was pretty much the most amazing concept I'd ever heard. Others like having money so they can spend it (I like this, too.). We want the ability to acquire houses, cars, clothes, travel, and other pleasures. Regardless of why you like to have money—to save or to spend—it can be problematic if money becomes our ultimate reliance or happiness. As much as I love to put money away, the Lord has opened my heart to the joy and privilege of giving it away. This desire is not natural to me, not something I was born with. In fact, Paul reveals very specifically how this desire comes about in our lives.

Look at verses 8:1,7. What had God given the Macedonians that enabled them to give so generously? _____

In verse 6 we find that Titus was the one who went to Corinth to help facilitate this collection for the poor in Jerusalem. The Corinthians were supposed to have been saving for this act of giving, which they'd been instructed to do in 1 Corinthians 16:1-4. What was Titus there to ensure?

Read verse 7. List the five areas Paul acknowledged the Corinthians excelled in, followed by a sixth action he wanted to make sure they didn't forget to complete. I filled in a couple for you.

1.

2.

3.

4. *Earnestness*

5. *Love*

6.

Now about the collection for the saints: You should do the same as I instructed the Galatian churches. On the first day of the week, each of you is to set something aside and save in keeping with how he prospers, so that no collections will need to be made when I come. When I arrive, I will send with letters those you recommend to carry your gracious gift to Jerusalem. If it is suitable for me to go as well, they can travel with me.
1 Corinithains 16:1-4, HCSB

Paul commended the Corinthians for succeeding in several areas, but wanted to make sure they didn't forget generous giving in the process. This tells me that you can love the Lord and excel in certain Christlike qualities and still miss the vital grace of generosity. As we make our way through chapters 8–9 over the next few days, we're going to record 11 truths about generosity. This will help us reframe the act of sacrificial giving from something we resist to one of the great privileges of our lives. Today we'll record the first two. After checking the correct word, record these statements in our "11 Truths About Generosity" on page 123.

1. God's definition of generous giving isn't dependent on how much or how little _____ a person has (8:2,12).

❏ *peace*　　　　　　　　　　❏ *wealth*
❏ *health*　　　　　　　　　　❏ *joy*

2. The experience of giving is a privilege that's accompanied by _____ even in difficult circumstances (8:2).

❏ *peace*　　　　　　　　　　❏ *wealth*
❏ *health*　　　　　　　　　　❏ *joy*

PERSONAL TAKE: *Why do you think Paul didn't command the Corinthians to give? (See verse 8. Also, look ahead at 9:7 for further information.)*

Do you remember the earlier theme of sincerity? One of my friends noted, "From the beginning we've learned about Paul's emphasis on the sincerity of faith. Here he doesn't command the Corinthians to give because he wants them to give out of their own free will, so the giving will be sincere. This is such a strong theme in the book I hadn't recognized before."

I'm always inspired by other believers who genuinely model the character of Christ. When Paul shared that the Macedonians were begging him for the privilege to give to the Jewish believers in Jerusalem, he was holding them up as a model for the Corinthians. The Macedonians were giving out of joy, not duty. Paul wanted the Corinthians to experience the same privilege and joy in their giving.

PERSONAL REFLECTION: *What Christlike quality have you been inspired to pursue because you first saw it in someone else?*

Other people can inspire us in great ways, but none like the person of Jesus. Write 2 Corinthians 8:9 below.

PERSONAL TAKE: *In what ways did Jesus become poor for you? In what ways have you been made rich because of Him? To better understand this, read Philippians 2:5-8.*

PERSONAL RESPONSE: *Read 2 Corinthians 8:9 as many times as you need for it to drop into your heart. Do you take the grace of Jesus for granted, or do you see His sacrificial gift as a privilege to emulate? Explain.*

Here's a truth that has recently convicted my heart: I have become less "rich" for people, but I have yet to become poor for anyone. It is one thing for me to skim off the top of my abundance, and another thing to scrape off a layer of my pleasures or savings. But it's something entirely different altogether to get down to the subterranean floor of all I have and give it to someone else that they might become rich. This is the way of Jesus. He was rich in that He shared in the privileges of equality with God (Phil. 2:6), the fullness of unbroken fellowship with the Father and Holy Spirit. He became poor by taking on our flesh, confining Himself to the limitations and suffering of this world, ultimately to death on a cross. And He did it to make us rich. Oh, dear sister, not rich in material stuff, because this can actually make us poor in matters of the spirit. But rich in peace that doesn't cut and run in the face of uncertainty. Rich in contentment that knows how to ride both the waves of abundance and slim pickings. Rich in intimacy with Him that oddly enough grows deeper and more precious in suffering's soil. Rich in joy whether by the gifts of material blessings that bring us a measure of happiness, or the joy that comes with giving our lives away. Rich in life—abundant and eternal.

Earlier in today's study we looked at a word found in 8:1,7 and now we see it again in verse 9. What was behind Jesus' giving up of His riches and becoming poor for us?

Our ability to be generous and to sacrificially give is directly related to God's grace.

Our ability to be generous and to sacrificially give is directly related to God's grace. We can't drum this up on our own. Take a few minutes and end today's study with prayer. Ask the Lord for more grace in your giving. Confess to Him your fears and excuses holding you back from being a generous giver. Ask Him for the opportunity to share in the privilege of coming alongside others with the gift of generosity. It's where the joy is.

DAY 4

DYNAMICS OF GIVING

2 CORINTHIANS 8:10-15

On a scale of 1-10, how excited are you to give money to your church, a ministry, or the poor? What if I told you that for the rest of your life you'd have enough money to buy everything you want, save as much as you want, invest as much as you want, and anything you gave away would be on top of your limitless supply of money? How excited would you be to give? In other words, if giving didn't actually require you to sacrifice in any way, would you be more excited to write that check or set aside that monthly tithe?

The reason I ask this question is that when challenged to give, we may be reluctant because of what giving will cost us. If I give $40 a month to sponsor a child, that's $40 less I have for lattes. If I tithe 10 percent of my income to my church, this chips away at my kids' college fund. If I make that one-time donation to a house for orphans I don't see how I'll be able to go on vacation. If I support that missionary for a year, I can't take advantage of this amazing investment opportunity. Bottom line, what makes giving so difficult is that when we give our money away, we're also giving up what that money can do for us.

You've probably heard people say things like, "Man, I wish I were independently wealthy so I could just give money away to people in need." This assumes three things that I don't think are true: First, if we were independently wealthy, we'd automatically give tons of money away. Second, we need to be financially set before we can give as freely as we want to. Third, the greater the amount of money we give, the more pleased God is with our giving. In today's passage, Paul is going to dismantle these assumptions as he encourages the Corinthians to give to the church in Jerusalem with passion and excitement.

READ 2 CORINTHIAN 8:10-15.

In verse 10, what motivated the Corinthians to give?
❏ *duty*   ❏ *desire*
❏ *a command*   ❏ *prayer*

True or False: *According to verses 11-12, the amount a person can give is what's most important to God.*

PERSONAL TAKE: *Why do you think Paul needed to remind them to complete the process of giving? I mean, if they had the desire to give wouldn't that naturally lead to fulfilling the gift?*

PERSONAL REFLECTION: *What causes a disconnect between your willingness to give and actually following through (e.g., forgetfulness, fear of the future, lack of planning)?*

Reread 2 Corinthians 8:13-15 and sum up the basic message in one sentence.

In verse 15, Paul quotes from the Book of Exodus about God's provision for the Israelites during their wilderness wanderings. Read Exodus 16:11-18 to get a better understanding of what Paul is talking about. Ultimately, how much did the people gather (Ex. 16:18)?

The Lord's provision of manna for the Israelites was a gift and also a test—He wanted to see if they would be obedient in trusting Him by not hoarding the manna overnight (except on the sixth day). The Lord had promised to consistently provide, day-by-day. The church at Corinth had a great deal more wealth and resources than the impoverished Jews in Jerusalem. It wouldn't be right for them to stockpile that wealth and stuff more rooms full of furniture and sail to extravagant vacations while their brothers and sisters could barely put food on the table. The Gentile Corinthians had; the Jerusalem Jews had not. Or is that totally accurate? Look again at verse 14.

After the Corinthians supplied the need of the Jews, what would in turn happen?

PERSONAL REFLECTION: *If the Corinthians were fairly well off and the Jews were significantly impoverished, what need would the Corinthians have and how could the Jews supply that need? Give this some thought.*

There are a few applications from this passage. One, practically speaking, there could come a time in the future when the economic tables would be turned. The Corinthian church could be in physical want and the Jerusalem church would financially provide for them. But also, theologically speaking, the Jews—special in God's sight as His chosen people—had already given to the Gentiles in the sense that their spiritual riches had been shared with them, actually with all of us. (See Rom. 15:26-27 in the margin.)

I believe additional layers of truth are also at work here. In a few days I'll be leaving for the Amazon in Brazil for Justice & Mercy International's Fifth Annual Jungle Pastor's Conference. By our standards, the hundred pastors and wives I'll spend the week with are immensely poor. Most live in huts, gather their own food, sleep in hammocks, and live on less than $100 month. But make no mistake, they will supply my need out of their abundance. They will melt my religious cynicism with the fire of their faith. The fullness of joy they have in knowing Jesus will inspire me to long for Him with more fervor. The way God is using them to spread the gospel down the Amazon will cast light on the silly, petty, flimsy things on which I spend energy. They will expose the needs I have outside of what my bank account can supply. I will supply their want and they mine. This is equality.

PERSONAL REFLECTION: *Describe a time when you gave sacrificially and ended up having one of your own needs supplied.*

> ... for Macedonia and Achaia were pleased to make a contribution for the poor among the saints in Jerusalem. Yes, they were pleased, and indeed are indebted to them. For if the Gentiles have shared in their spiritual benefits, then they are obligated to minister to Jews in material needs.
> Romans 15:26-27, HCSB

We've learned three more concepts about giving to add to our list of 11. See below. Write these on page 123.

3. Our willingness to give must be matched with actual follow-through (8:11).

4. God cares more about our desire to give than the amount we're able to give (8:12). (See also Mark 12:41-44.)

5. The discipline of giving is for the mutual benefit of the giver and the receiver (8:14).

PERSONAL RESPONSE: *Which of these three truths is the most eye-opening to you, and how will it affect your giving?*

I can't tell you how many times I've wanted to give to a ministry or tithe to my church but let the moment pass me by. It's the strangest thing that somehow I can get all my credit card information entered online before the one-day sale ends for that duvet cover, but I can put off sending that check to my church. I won't forget to bring my gift card to the nail salon but I'll forget to bring my checkbook to that ministry fund raiser. Anyone else? Anyone?

Giving is a gateway to joy.

I'm hoping we've allowed the Holy Spirit to reframe our view of giving so we'll see it as a privilege as opposed to a duty. After all, giving is a gateway to joy. My prayer is that we'll see it through this lens, then find ourselves wanting to give as eagerly as we used to want to save or spend.

DAY 5
IN THIS TOGETHER

2 CORINTHIANS 8:16-24

We really are in this together. No one can save the world alone. Whether we're organizing a fund raiser, raising a family, fighting human trafficking, building a church in a developing country, in the process of adopting, or being sent as a missionary—we need each other. We need the collective manpower and the assortment of gifts the Lord has given each of us working together. We also need accountability, the checks and balances that ensure that when success transpires no one's head gets too big for the door. Any time money is involved, especially for charitable purposes, responsible people are essential for safeguarding and directing its use. We need one another for mutual encouragement when ministry results are slim, for prayer when we've run out of spunk. Some people will need to stay and manage the foundation while others will be called to go and pioneer new territory. No matter what piece God has given you to steward, be certain that your gift is essential to the whole and when you bring it forth you will not be alone.

READ 2 CORINTHIANS 8:16-24.

Titus was eager, full of enthusiasm to run forward with this project. I have to admit, I don't always have this intense passion for ministry. I want to desire others above myself and get more excited about someone coming to know Christ than I get over a new sofa. But too often our fleshly hearts beat for the things of the world, don't they? So how do we get the passion of a Paul, Titus, or the unnamed brothers mentioned in this passage?

> *Verse 16 reminds me of a favorite passage from Nehemiah. Both texts give us a peek into the answer. Look up Nehemiah 2:11-12 and in the space below compare it to 2 Corinthians 8:16. From where does a passion to serve others come?*

I love that God gave Titus the same passion for the Corinthians that He'd given Paul. When God breaks our hearts and the hearts of our spiritual community for the same cause, it ignites a shared passion. A bonfire of activity crackles and whistles, and we bond around its warmth. We suddenly

have ministry stuff to talk about that's more exciting than church gossip, more fulfilling than a marathon day of television. My mom just texted me a picture of herself and two of her girlfriends, Jean and Cheryl, putting together hand-sewn gift bags of makeup and beautifying products for the pastor's wives I'm about to see in the Amazon. My mom went to the jungle two years in a row, and now she wants to contribute in a different way—from a place without the heat and roaches. I get it. Some stay; some go. Some sew floral bags and put lipstick in them; others deliver those bags. This is what we call teamwork.

Think of the people who share the same desire God's given you for the poor, lost, or hurting (or any people group, really). Write what you love most about sharing in ministry with them.

PERSONAL RESPONSE: *Verse 17 implies that Titus eagerly responded to Paul's request to travel to Corinth and oversee the collection of this offering for the Jews. Understandably, we can't take every ministry opportunity that comes along, and sometimes wisdom means saying no to something good. That said, is there a current opportunity for you to be involved in a ministry that you've turned down for the wrong reasons? (Think selfishness, insecurity, pride, fear, competitiveness, etc.) Take a moment to lay this opportunity before the Lord with a heart willing to be obedient to His call.*

Delegation can be tough for leaders because we don't always want to hand over control. We have a specific way we do things. And what happens if we delegate to someone who uses a different translation of the Bible or a different brand of computer? But notice that even the great apostle Paul entrusted ministry opportunities to others. He needed capable, gifted people to step up around him.

You may not be in vocational ministry like Paul, but all of us are called to disciple others and raise up future mothers, teachers, leaders, homemakers in the Lord. Take a moment to ask the Lord to show you a Titus in your life that you can mentor and invest in.

Two "brothers" are mentioned in this passage but they're not given names. What is said about each of them?

• First brother (vv. 18-19)

• Second brother (v. 22)

Paul takes great pains to avoid any criticism over how this offering is administered (vv. 21-22). We all know that anytime a large sum of money is involved, people scrutinize and possibly question how it's being handled.

Knowing this, Paul not only made sure he was acting rightly in the Lord's eyes, but also in the eyes of _____ (v. 21).

As we close the week, I want to spend a moment on two verses we could easily gloss over. Reread verses 23-24. Why do you think Paul took the time to put an extra stamp of approval on Titus and these brothers?

I've grown up in the church. Literally. When I was five days old, my mom and dad carted me into the building that the church they founded met in. (That was before newfangled ideas came about like keeping newborns away from church people with colds.) Throughout my years in the church, I've seen the body of Christ work wonders like no other entity on earth. I've also seen—and shamefully admit I've been a part of—gossip, criticism, and negative critique of leadership. Pastors and church leaders need our encouragement. They need the benefit of the doubt sometimes. We need to cut them some slack. Remember, they're meeting a thousand needs at a time. Often, when something looks like favoritism, pride, or manipulation it may simply be that we're not seeing the whole picture.

Paul knew the Corinthians may not be accepting of Titus or these other brothers—they'd hardly been accepting of Paul himself. So he gently reminded them to show Titus and his friends the _____ of their love.
❏ *intentions*   ❏ *wisdom*
❏ *hope*   ❏ *proof*

PERSONAL RESPONSE: *As you think of your church's ministry leaders, what is one way you can show them the proof of your love this week? We can waste so much time talking about how things could be better or what the leadership isn't doing for us, but none of this amounts to anything profitable. Let's prove our love to our ministry leaders who serve us so tirelessly. They are literally, as Paul put it, "the glory of Christ" (v. 23).*

We now have two more truths about generosity to add to our list on page 123.

REVIEW VERSES 8:20-21.

6. Giving must be done in the right spirit but also in the right way.

We've already noted that several churches were involved in this endeavor to help the church in Jerusalem. In addition to Paul, Titus and two other brothers were also helping.

7. A lifestyle of generosity is not an individual endeavor but a team effort (8:16-24).

I have a heart to see ministry accomplished, but I'm painfully aware of the areas I lack in to accomplish that ministry. This is one of the reasons I love teamwork in the body of Christ. I'm grateful to work with people whose skills, personalities, and spiritual gifts are different from mine. Not only do I cherish their friendships, but also they make up for my lack—and hopefully I make up for theirs. The problem is that we're sometimes threatened by other people's strengths, especially in areas where we're weak. We may not understand people who are simply different from us, which can lead us to judge and eschew instead of appreciate and links arms with. So at the close of this week's study, let's look to enjoy and embrace the gifts and personalities of others. Let's encourage each other and work together. We have a world that desperately needs Christ's body to serve in unity. Let's create space for our collective giftedness by laying aside our insecurities—a spiritually and physically hungry world will be so thankful we did.

The problem is that we're sometimes threatened by other people's strengths, especially in areas where we're weak.

11 TRUTHS ABOUT GENEROSITY

1.

2.

3.

4.

5.

6.

7.

8.

9.

10.

11.

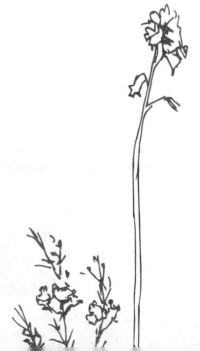

SESSION 5 VIEWER GUIDE

RETHINKING GENEROSITY

GROUP DISCUSSION:

Why is giving to our brothers and sisters one of the greatest privileges we'll ever have? Is that the way you view giving? Explain.

Is sacrificial generosity a characteristic of your life? Explain.

What is your motivation to give? Why is motivation so important when it comes to giving?

Kelly said "God's definition of giving richly has nothing to do with your wealth." Do you really believe that? Explain.

What's the difference in becoming less rich for people versus becoming poor for them?

What one thing stood out for you from this video?

Sausage and Butternut Squash Risotto (serves 6)

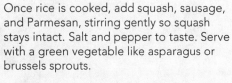

INGREDIENTS:

Ingredients	
1 large butternut squash, seeded, cubed (about 4 cups)	I have friends who are missionaries in Milan, Italy, and when I visited them my friend Nina whipped up this dish. While I can't make it taste exactly like she did—I think for truly exquisite sausage the pigs need to be Italian pigs— it's still one of the biggest hits I've put on the table and it will easily feed a crowd. You're going to love me (and Nina) for this one.
1 tablespoon olive oil	
salt and freshly ground pepper	
1 pound ground sausage (remove casings if needed)	
2 tablespoons butter	
1 onion, diced	
16 ounces Arborio rice (or any firm short-grain rice)	
5 cups chicken stock (or more)	
½ cup grated Parmesan cheese	

DIRECTIONS

Preheat oven to 425 degrees. Toss cubed butternut squash with 1 tablespoon of olive oil, salt, and pepper in a bowl. Place on baking sheet. Roast for 20 to 25 minutes until edges are lightly browned.

While squash cooks, brown ground sausage in a pan, breaking up with a wooden spoon. Drain most of the fat, keeping a small amount for flavor, and set aside.

In a large saucepan, sauté onion with butter over medium heat for 3 minutes. Add rice and stir until well coated, about 2 minutes. Add 1 cup of stock and stir constantly until absorbed. Do this with each cup, waiting until stock is absorbed before adding the next cup. After 5 cups, if you feel like you can still add more liquid, add ½ cup of water (or stock) at a time until the rice is creamy and the texture is to your liking.

Once rice is cooked, add squash, sausage, and Parmesan, stirring gently so squash stays intact. Salt and pepper to taste. Serve with a green vegetable like asparagus or brussels sprouts.

SESSION 6

OUR MINISTRY ASSIGNMENTS

Aunthood is a bit like motherhood without the day-to-day responsibilities and college tuition bills. It's a little like being a grandmother but with a smidge more youth. For me, being an aunt has been a lovely surprise. Not the actual day it happened—I had nine months to anticipate the event—but the unexpected joy into which it has so wonderfully evolved.

Aunthood crept up on me.

These little creatures kept springing into the world, crawling into my house, then strutting through the kitchen demanding juice boxes. Suddenly, there were five of them. Actual humans. All with distinct personalities, cherubic cheeks, and germs. Most of them are now in school, having flung me out there as a single branch on their kindergarten family trees—a precious bough I alone hold in each of their lives. They've given me a place, and they've given me stories.

I remember when Holland, my youngest niece, was born. Her 6-year-old sister Maryn's excitement bubbled over with sisterly zeal. She was now old enough to snuggle a real-life doll who cooed and made smacking noises with her button mouth. Emmett, who was four at the time, was not nearly as amused. For him, visiting Holland in the hospital during those first few days was a real yawner.

Incidentally, Emmett's parts of speech were in the throes of development. He routinely switched the pronoun "she" for "hers," and always used the plural. As in,

"Mom, hers is really bothering me." "Mom, will you tell hers to stop." So when Emmett was told the family was going to visit his newborn sister in the hospital, for the second day in a row, his response was, "We have to go see hers again?"

When my sister, Katie, was released from the hospital her husband, Brad, picked her and Holland up, and their newly enlarged family headed straight to collect Maryn and Emmett from school. They skipped across the schoolyard, and Emmett punched the button that opens the side door to the minivan. Methodically it slid open inch-by-inch, just like it always did, only this time newborn Holland was taking up a seat in the car. Emmett lamented with utter shock, "You mean HERS is still here?"

"Buddy, get in the car," Brad said. "Hers is going to be here for the rest of your life."

I've never forgotten this because most of us can relate. We've had that moment when we realize, for better or worse, we are stuck with a certain person or people or church congregation. Maybe it's the result of our own choosing or maybe it's what we discovered on the other side of the car door

when we had no choice but to step through. None of us are exempt from having to get along with trying family members, working through complicated relationship triangles, or quirky church dynamics. We've all had that moment of realization that despite how tired and beat up we may be, hers is still here. And perhaps not going anywhere.

The stamina of affection can only carry you so far. Sometimes the only thing keeping us in the race are the endorphins of pure calling.

This is where the final few chapters of 2 Corinthians shoot into the sky with a bang. The difficult false teachers and confused congregants of Corinth don't seem to be going anywhere, and the attacks on Paul aren't ceasing. In the middle of a rather combustible environment, Paul stays with them. He continues to fight for the relationship. I keep thinking about these Corinthians and how my propensity would have been to clap the dust off my hands and move onto another city. To find a more grateful bunch of believers who would be happy to have someone with the spiritual accolades of the apostle Paul as their spiritual father. Surely other churches in other cities would have been more appreciative. But you know what it came down to? A calling.

This week we'll see that Corinth was part of an assignment God had given Paul. It was smack in a sphere in which God had commissioned him to serve. Yes, Paul loved the Corinthians deeply, but the stamina of affection can only carry you so far. Sometimes the only thing keeping us in the race are the endorphins of pure calling. I don't know who you're called to care for but my hunch is that a few of them may be wearing you out. Maybe you're not feeling appreciated, or they seem disinterested, or you fear you're being taken advantage of, or they keep slipping back into old patterns. This is when you press in, step up, push back, stay engaged. Why? Because you've been called.

The relentless commitment to stay in there that Paul demonstrated with the Corinthians is a trait I want more of. But this trait is hewn over the long haul as we choose not to abandon a group of people just because things have gotten hard. Or aren't what they used to be. Or because hers is still here.

As we enter this week together, I have a prayer for you: that Christ's love will compel you to stay committed in those trying relationships. When you're tempted to draw harsh judgment from your scabbard, instead draw humble authority and use it to build up rather than tear down. I pray you won't lose the pure desire for people that can easily blur into desiring their possessions or what they can do for you. I pray the Holy Spirit gives you discernment to know when to be soft-spoken and when to be bold, when to let an offense roll off your back and when to confront. As you fulfill the ministry assignment the Lord has given you, may you view the people in your spheres no longer from a human perspective, but as in Christ (2 Cor. 5:16-17). He can make even the most challenging person brand new. Even *hers*.

DAY 1
HELD ACCOUNTABLE

2 CORINTHIANS 9:1-5

When I step back from the intricacies of 2 Corinthians I see the letter as one resounding bell hearkening us to the adventure of a life of ministry. No believer is exempt. Every one of us has an assignment from the Lord to be used of Him. That concept, being used by the Lord, is one I've known since childhood. But last week while plodding up a hillside in Brazil with my friend Milton, whose first language is Portuguese, I was reminded of this honor. His English is impeccable, but occasionally he misses a nuance by a thread, making the expression especially memorable. He was talking about what a blessing it is to be useful to God. His phrase "useful to God" instead of "used by God," caused the meaning to hit me anew: what a privilege to have our time, talents, resources, experience, education, personality, and heart made useful to God.

Dear sister, this has been one of the greatest privileges and honors of my life: to be useful in God's hands. When we choose to align ourselves with God and His ways, however imperfectly, He sovereignly gathers the darkest seasons and woeful failures of our past, transforms them and makes us, well, useful in His kingdom. To God be the glory! I know what some of you are thinking *God doesn't need us*. True, He is all-powerful and "is not served by human hands, as if he needed anything" (Acts 17:25). At the same time, in His sovereignty He has called us to be co-laborers with Him, given us spiritual gifts unique to each of us, and commanded us to go and tell everyone we know about the good news. Consider the unrivaled privilege of being useful to God.

I'm so excited to dive into chapter 9 with you. This passage continues our emphasis on a lifestyle of generosity, one of the ways God uses our lives to bless others. Before we jump into the reading, let's review some facts we learned last week (you can look back for help).

Where was the poor church that would receive the offering Paul and his friends were collecting? _____

What other significantly poor church was giving out of her poverty to the aforementioned impoverished church? _____

Who had Paul sent to oversee this offering? Titus and the

_____.

READ 2 CORINTHIANS 9:1-5.

If the Corinthians were so eager to give, why did Paul send the brothers ahead of the collection?

I've noticed a trend over the past decade or so: People increasingly do not like to be managed or answer to authority. More than ever, it seems, we esteem independence and the idea that we shouldn't have to answer to anybody. Never mind that living outside of authority is actually not freedom at all. In the case of the Corinthians, Paul wanted to make sure they followed through on their plan to give. He didn't want to be ashamed of them or for them to be ashamed of themselves in front of the Macedonians. This meant the process needed some oversight. The Corinthians needed accountability.

PERSONAL RESPONSE: *The visit to check up on the Corinthians could have been offensive to the church or welcomed, depending on their attitude. How open are you to being held accountable? Do you get defensive when people speak into your life or want to keep up with your spiritual growth? Explain.*

My friend Julie pointed out that when Paul's friends visited Corinth it wasn't to pressure the Corinthians to give more, but to simply urge them to do what they said they would do. It was a call to integrity and responsibility.

Last week we read about how the Macedonian church had inspired the church at Corinth to give to the Jerusalem church (2 Cor. 8:1-5). Now it's the other way around. The generosity of Achaia (surrounding area of Corinth) had stirred up the Macedonian church with eager excitement to give (v. 2).

PERSONAL REFLECTION: *Who inspires you to give passionately and eagerly? What is it about them that stirs up this passion?*

Look back at 2 Corinthians 8:11. What needed to match the Corinthians' readiness or eagerness to give?

There's a difference between a readiness of intention and a readiness of completion.[1] I've had lots of great intentions over the years, but I've not always had the same resolve to bring that readiness to fulfillment. I can't tell you how many times I've left the Amazon thinking, *I need to learn Portuguese*, then life crowds out my intentions. We can hear an inspiring testimony at church and decide we want to give to that person's ministry, but by the time we drive home we've settled back into the demands of our lifestyle and bank accounts, and the moment is lost. Or maybe we've been invited to give our time in an ongoing way. In the moment we're ready to go, but then the television shows and the weekly dinner dates with friends tug at our time, and we forgo the opportunity to serve. Paul knew the Corinthians needed help completing a task they were inspired to begin. And we do, too.

> **PERSONAL REFLECTION:** *Think of the last time you were really excited to give toward something but for some reason never did. What happened? What got in the way? How can you incorporate a measure of accountability to help fulfill your intentions to give? Be specific.*

The detail given to the planning and administration of this large gift to the Jerusalem church encourages me. It makes me grateful for accountants, administrators, and other people who love a spreadsheet. It helps me appreciate the ones who give their time to be overseers like Titus and the brothers. Most of the time money doesn't appear out of nowhere for good causes; it has to be raised. And it doesn't magically distribute itself; it has to be overseen. The church of Corinth had great intentions to give but fulfilling those intentions required planning and accountability. We need the same structure for our giving.

> **PERSONAL TAKE:** *According to 2 Corinthians 9:5, why do you think planning ahead for the collection would keep the gift from being given grudgingly?*

For our eighth truth in our "11 Truths about Generosity," turn to page 123 and write the following:

8. A lifestyle of generous giving requires planning.

In verse 9:5 Paul wanted to make sure the gift would be ready. Take a journey with me to another part of Scripture. Read Luke 12:32-40 where Jesus spoke about us being ready for His return.

Your Bible may have a break between verses 34 and 35. Perhaps it's because of this break that I never noticed the connection between giving to the poor and being _____ for Jesus' return.

❏ *Excited*　　　　　　　❏ *Sleeping*
❏ *Serving*　　　　　　　❏ *Ready*

PERSONAL TAKE: *How does being consumed by our material possessions keep us from being ready for Christ's return? Give this some thought.*

Look back at Luke 12:35. I loved researching the different translations of this verse.

NIV: Be dressed ready for service and keep your lamps burning.

KJV: Let your loins be girded about, and your lights burning.

ESV: Stay dressed for action, and keep your lamps burning.

HCSB: Be ready for service and have your lamps lit.

MSG (paraphrase): Keep your shirts on; keep the lights on!

The idea is clear that when Jesus returns He longs to find His children in the game. The lights will be on because we're not taking a nap from our Christianity or frolicking in the darkness of sin. We're not in our pajamas binge-watching the television or binge-surfing the internet, and we're not naked in our shame that forever keeps us hidden in the covers of uselessness. No! All things have been made new. Jesus has fulfilled the law and given us the grace to live in His power. We're new creatures, and we must evidence the newness He's brought about in our hearts. So get your clothes on, lace up your shoes, and, as my friend says to me before watching a big college football game, get your ankles taped.

PERSONAL RESPONSE: *Considering Jesus' return, describe one way you can dress yourself for action, and one way you can keep the lights on.*

The truth is we're not going to be generous by accident. Tithing to our churches, giving above and beyond to a ministry, or helping a family member or friend will not magically happen. We have to prepare for it, plan for it, pray over it, and ultimately execute it. Let's bring our good intentions to effective completions. A lost world is waiting. And, who knows, it may be in the middle of our giving that our Master returns and finds us just as He'd always dreamed: ready.

The truth is we're not going to be generous by accident.

DAY 2
SOWING GENEROUSLY

2 CORINTHIANS 9:6-15

Charles Spurgeon said, "We want personal consecration. I have heard that word pronounced *'purse and all* consecration,' a most excellent pronunciation certainly. He who loves Jesus consecrates to him all that he has, and feels it a delight that he may lay anything at the feet of Him who laid down his life for us."[2] Who doesn't love some Charles Spurgeon wit? I knew after all this talk of generosity you'd appreciate some "purse and all" humor. But how true that offering our money and possessions to the Lord is not meant to make us heartsick; rather it's to be a delight!

We'll witness this as we finish chapter 9, one of my favorite passages in all of the Bible. It needs no introduction.

READ 2 CORINTHIANS 9:6-15.

What concept from this passage speaks to you the most? Why?

We'll discover the remaining three truths about generosity in today's passage. Let's look first at numbers 9 and 10.

Based on verse 6, check the correct statement below and write it as #9 on the list on page 123.
❏ *The amount you reap has nothing to do with the amount you sow.*
❏ *The amount you reap is proportionate to the amount you sow.*
❏ *The amount you reap doesn't matter.*

According to verse 7: God loves a _____ giver. List this statement as #10 on page 123.

At the time of this writing, the steeled soil of winter is about to surrender to spring's verdant sod. I'm sharpening my spade. Under winter's reign my raised beds are but a pile of dead vines and stalks wrapped in each other's arms, dreading the fate that awaits them in the compost pile. I should have tossed them in there months ago, but you know, life. At any rate, once the beds get cleaned and spring springs, it will be time to sow. If I tuck my seeds into the ground liberally, I will reap in equal measure. If I do so sparingly, I will harvest in like and meager quantity. But something else will also determine my harvest: what I've *decided* to sow.

Paul mentions in verse 7 that deciding how much to give is the precursor to actually giving. Every good gardener knows that planting a garden requires decision making ahead of time. What will I plant? How much will I plant? Where will I plant? You don't just start tossing seeds out there without a plan—I did this once, and we can talk about how that turned out later. So I want you to consider what decisions God is leading you to. Here are some questions to help you get started:

1. Do you regularly give to your church? If not, why not? Determine what's keeping you from giving, lay those reasons or excuses before God, and ask Him what amount to give on a consistent basis.

2. Do you have a surplus over and above your tithe that you can give to a specific need in your church, a ministry, or an individual? How will you determine when and where to give it?

3. Is God asking you to give something that may not be measured in dollars and cents? It may be offering a room in your house, donating your time or your expertise, lending a rental property, or employing someone. If any of this resonates with you, decide what the next step should be to obey the Lord.

> **PERSONAL REFLECTION:** *Which of these three questions challenges you the most? Why? What steps will you take to be obedient?*

READ 2 CORINTHIANS 9:8:

And God is able to bless you abundantly, so that in all things at all times, having all that you need, you will abound in every good work.

Using this translation, fill in the following:

God makes all grace abound to the cheerful giver so that

   In all _____

       At all _____

           I will have all I_____

I know few greater joys than giving by faith and watching the Lord provide all I need in ways I couldn't have imagined, filling wants I didn't know I had, blessing me with more than I could have known. This is why this passage is one of my favorites. It's been said that you can't out-give God. It's true. Because giving back is His specialty. He blesses us in the most remarkable ways when we give, hardly ever dollar for dollar. Generosity in God's kingdom isn't a karma-based system—praise the Lord! It's way more personal, dynamic, and creative than that. Look back at the NIV translation of 2 Corinthians 9:8 and note the ultimate purpose of giving.

In all things, at all times, we have everything we need so we can abound in what?
❏ *happiness*
❏ *security*
❏ *wealth*
❏ *every good work*

You may have been secretly hoping that verse 8 ended with having all you need so you could abound in material wealth. I know the feeling. But what Paul tells us here is nothing short of revelation. When we give generously God promises to give us everything we need for the good works He's created us for. This is by far the greater blessing. You were created to have impact on this earth for God's kingdom. I don't know what works He's called you to, but I know they're good ones that will have eternal results. And I promise, you don't want to miss them for whatever temporal desire you're clinging to. He has something for you to do that will fulfill your heart, mind, and senses exponentially more than money or more stuff. And whatever that something is, it's good.

> *You were created to have impact on this earth for God's kingdom.*

PERSONAL REFLECTION: *How does God equipping the cheerful giver for good works inspire and encourage you?*

In verse 9, Paul quotes from the Psalms. Read Psalm 112. What is the most meaningful concept to you from this passage?

What strikes me about the generous man in Psalm 112 is this person's lack of fear. It can be said of the woman who lives by these truths that she can freely give because she's not dependent upon her money to secure her future. She can scatter her gifts to the poor because she doesn't need those gifts to garner friends or prop up her reputation—she trusts God for that. She's not living for the temporary nature of wealth. She is steadfast in the Lord. Money is not her comfort.

So why is it that having money seems to make us less afraid? In our culture one of the most popular words to follow the word *financial* is *security*. Who hasn't lain in bed at night worried about how a child will get through college,

or a medical bill will be met, or what will happen if the job is terminated, or I can't pay my employees? We think if we just had the money, all would be well. But that thinking puts our hope in something that Scripture says will sprout wings and fly away (Prov. 23:5). The provision of money can be a wonderful blessing from God, but it can never take the place of God.

The provision of money can be a wonderful blessing from God, but it can never take the place of God.

> *Consider 2 Corinthians 9:10-11. Where does our seed for sowing and bread for eating come from?*

In a world of grocery store shelves overflowing with options, it's easy to forget that God is the source of our seed and bread. Our tables would be empty without Him. When I stop and remember that all I have comes from God, it inspires me to give more freely. I trust Him, knowing that all I have is ultimately His, and He has the power to replenish my supply.

> *List our final truth about generosity on page 123 with this statement:*

11. God is the ultimate Source of our giving (9:8-10).

> *What kind of harvest does God promise us in verse 10?*

> *What is the purpose of being made rich in every way according to verse 11?*

In some ways it seems strange that the reward for the Corinthian's generous giving of their material resources would result in spiritual blessings (harvest of righteousness). But I believe a wonderful truth is at work. Anytime we give generously of our material possessions, the Lord blesses us. Sometimes this comes in the form of financial blessings, but it always comes in the form of spiritual blessings. And don't make the mistake of thinking that the spiritual blessings are less exciting or desirable than the financial ones. The privilege of being part of an eternal harvest of righteousness, without end, is one of the greatest joys and adventures of our earthly lives.

> **PERSONAL REFLECTION:** *What harvest of righteousness in your life has been most meaningful to you? Why? (Consider anything that resembles spiritual prosperity: someone you led to Christ, raising your kids to love Jesus, the effects of a mission trip you took, someone you disciple, etc.)*

Review verses 11-12,15, and note what all this generosity resulted in.

PERSONAL REFLECTION: *When Paul says in verse 12 that the Corinthians were supplying the needs of the Jews, the word* supplying *literally means to fill up something that is lacking. Briefly write about a time when someone's generosity filled up something lacking in your life?*

What was one way the Jews "paid back" the Corinthians in verse 14?

As I meditate on these final verses of chapter 9, I'm deeply moved by the relational aspect of giving. The Corinthians had the high privilege of supplying a church as special as the Jerusalem church with something they desperately needed. In return, the Jerusalem church responded with deep affection and prayers for the Corinthians. And all this overflowed in thanksgiving and praise to God. Sharing, by its very nature, is relational, whether you're giving to me or I'm giving to you. And if it's within the bonds of Christ we'll be thanking and praising God together, which adds a third person into our fellowship. If greed separates, then generosity brings together.

If greed separates, then generosity brings together.

We know from other portions of Scripture that the Lord promises to take care of our needs (shelter, food, clothing—Matt. 6:25-33), and often He goes over and above with financial blessings. Money and material possessions can be tremendous gifts. But our passion should be to honor the Lord by using those gifts to bless others. Right now there's someone whose supply is lacking in an area in which you are full. And more than likely the reverse is true. It's the nature of this business of needing one another.

Will you generously fill up what is lacking by giving where God is calling you to give? Will you take the time to make a decision about what you will give and when? You can't imagine who might in turn praise God for your obedience or who might realize the gospel is real because you put your money where your faith is. And, perhaps, most amazing of all, you won't begin to know what prayers might be prayed on your behalf when the recipient of your generosity praises God for you. This is what happens when we give God "purse and all."

DAY 3
TEARING DOWN WALLS

2 CORINTHIANS 10:1-6

Today we begin a new section of 2 Corinthians that will carry us through the end of the letter. You'll remember the first section began with the encouragement of God's comfort (1:1-11). From there Paul clarified why he needed to delay his visit to Corinth while addressing a few other issues in the church (1:12–2:13). Paul went on to explain and defend new covenant ministry, then resumed his travel narrative (2:14–7:16). After praising those who had been faithful in the church, he encouraged them to resume giving to the poor in Jerusalem (8:1–9:15). Moving forward, we'll predominantly read about Paul addressing the obstinate minority trying to take over the church in Corinth. Whether these were false teachers, blatant unbelievers, or those confused in the church, Paul was addressing them head on.

You'll notice chapters 10–13 signal a shift in tone. This has led some scholars to believe these chapters are actually a separate letter, though there's plenty of reason to believe they're part of the whole of 2 Corinthians. This is outside the scope of our study, but I want you to have some reference for why the tone of the letter turns a bit more confrontational. The key is to remember that Paul has turned his attention to some specific enemies who were looking to dominate the church by false teaching.

Part of the disruption in the church included some members who specifically attacked Paul for being weak and unimpressive in person. They accused him of putting forth a false image of strength in his letters, while perceiving him to be timid and waffling in person. Paul will explain he's anything but weak because of God's divine power at work in his life. Moreover, he's going to reveal that the weapons the world uses—and that we're often tempted to use—are paltry in comparison to this divine power we have in Christ.

READ 2 CORINTHIANS 10:1-6.

In verse 3, Paul reminds us that though we live in the world, we don't _____ like the world does?

❏ *party*   ❏ *wage war*
❏ *live*   ❏ *behave*

According to verse 4, we use different _____ than the world.
- ❏ *tools*
- ❏ *weapons*
- ❏ *ingredients*
- ❏ *methods*

We know by now that Paul loves a good word picture. Warfare imagery would have been especially familiar to the culture of Paul's day, as Roman soldiers were common in the Mediterranean area. What may not be as obvious to us is that the warfare Paul referenced was a certain type of ancient battle called *siege warfare*. And siege warfare specifically focused on—you're going to love this—tearing down walls.[3] Anyone need some walls torn down in their lives? In the life of someone you love? Anyone as excited as I am about this imagery?

At the top of chapter 10, we find Paul ready to tear down the walls of anti-Christian thinking some outsiders had brought to the church at Corinth. Their teachings opposed the gospel and criticized Paul's apostolic authority. This had the potential to create a barrier between Paul and the church, but even worse, to turn the church to rely on a false gospel. Paul wasn't going to deal with these false teachers with earthly weapons because at their core the attacks weren't earthly in nature—they were spiritual onslaughts comprised of false thinking set against God.

PERSONAL REFLECTION: *Is there a current situation in your life where you're trying to fight a spiritual battle with worldly weapons? How have you found this to be ineffective?*

We've already noted that the believers' weapons of warfare are entirely different from fleshly earthly weapons. Since Paul's detractors were judging him for being weak, a sufferer, timid, and poor, we can assume some of the weapons they may have been looking for him to fight with were wealth, prestige, political power, pomp, wittiness, deceit, flatteries, manipulations, and so forth.

Most of us can't relate to being in the military on the front line of a battle; however, we've all experienced the battles of a different realm. We've come up against the brick walls of jealousy, anger, betrayal, arrogant coworkers, controlling bosses, broken marriages, wayward children, hurtful friendships. We've scaled a quarter of the way up the rampart of depression, overwhelming emotions, sexual sin, addiction, and paralyzing fear, only to lose our footing and skin ourselves to the bone on the slide back down. We know these battles well. They're the ones that require a full-on siege, but not with the weapons we hold in our hands or find in the self-help aisle.

According to the end of verse 4, what can we demolish with God's power?

❏ addictions   ❏ strongholds

❏ sin   ❏ emotions

Because today's text includes a number of significant words, we're going to look at some original Greek words and their definitions to understand their meanings. I'm looking forward to turning over these rocks with you and seeing what's underneath. Today's text is amazing!

The first piece of good news is that we have the power to demolish strongholds. The Greek word is *ochyrōma* and it can mean *(1) a castle, stronghold, fortress, fastness,* as well as *(2) anything on which one relies.* In ancient battle, if an opposing army wanted to overtake a city it had to conquer that city's fortress. If the army could get to the stronghold of the castle, it could capture the whole city. In verse 5, Paul's goes on to describe what these spiritual strongholds consist of.

> *According to verse 5, what's the first stronghold we have the power to demolish?*

The Greek word is *logismos,* and it means *thoughts, calculations, reasonings, reflections.*[4] I especially like scholar George Guthrie's explanation of these arguments: "walls of wrong thinking that stand in opposition to right Christian teaching."[5]

> *What's the second stronghold we're to tear down (v. 5)?*

We demolish arguments and every pretension that sets itself up against the knowledge of God, and we take captive every thought to make it obedient to Christ.
2 Corinthians 10:5

The Greek word for *pretension/high thing* is *hypsōma.* It denotes an elevated structure, i.e. barrier, rampart, bulwark. The impression here is that something other than or contrary to God has been raised up, lifted high with the purpose to intimidate.

So many of our problems and struggles can be traced back to our thinking. Consider these familiar expressions: "it's in your head," "don't overthink it," "the power of positive thinking," and "mind over matter." Because we know so much of the battle is in our minds, we think if we could just control our thoughts we could get a handle on things. But we also know this is much harder than it sounds. Sometimes it's harder because we're making it so! I excel at making things more difficult for myself than they need to be. How do I accomplish such brilliant feats, you ask? By sometimes believing—and even embracing—thoughts that are contrary to God's Word.

We have a problematic ability to compartmentalize our wrong thinking and our sin. Just yesterday I sat with a friend who wants to start Bible school, make more time to be involved in church, and study theology. He also just moved in with his girlfriend and spent a good part of our conversation trying to justify that decision. He used all kinds of arguments for why he thought this was a good idea, even though he knows what Scripture tells us about the beauty of marital commitment versus the more casual nature of cohabitation. Please know that my heart is tender toward my friend. But I simply have discovered the hard way that any thinking that sets itself up against God's Word and His ways only leads to heartache and pain. We must align our thinking with the mind of the Lord because our behavior follows our thinking.

Any thinking that sets itself up against God's Word and His ways only leads to heartache and pain.

Now that we know what walls need demolishing (arguments contrary to the Lord along with high, antagonistic pretensions) we need to remember the weapons we have are divine and mighty in power (v. 4). The Greek word for *power* is *dynatos*.

What word does this remind you of?

When it comes to tearing down these seemingly immovable walls, it's extraordinarily hopeful to know we can pull them down with a power by which the word *dynamite* derived its name. No matter what wall is towering over you, you are not powerless in Jesus.

But there is another step after tearing down wrong thinking with God's power. According to the second half of verse 5, what are we to take captive and make obedient to Christ?

In the original language, the phrase *take captive* means *to take as prisoner of war*.[6] In Paul's case, this meant that once he demolished the strongholds of false teaching, he was going to lead the Corinthians' thinking in the ways of Christ.

Verse 5 might be familiar to you and you may be thinking, *I've tried that—it doesn't work*. First, ask the Holy Spirit to show you this concept in a fresh way. Second, pay attention to the order in this passage.

1. We can't very well make our thoughts obedient to Jesus if we haven't first torn down the fortress of false beliefs (arguments/pretensions) that protects those thoughts. (Blatant, unrepentant sin will also keep that wall impenetrable). We can only become aware of our false beliefs when we compare them to the truths of Scripture. Once we can see the stronghold we attack it with Scripture memory, meditating on passages that speak against the lies on which the stronghold is built. Prayer is also essential. We pray privately and with others, asking God to supernaturally tear down each piece.

2. Once the central wall has been demolished we then take the negative thoughts that wall was protecting and make them obedient to Christ. I do this by confessing my wrong thinking to the Lord and asking Him to bring my thoughts in alignment with His truth. I also confide in trusted friends who will speak His truth to me.

3. We make sure our obedience is complete rather than partial. After I've confessed any wrong thinking and any harmful actions that resulted from that thinking, I determine to walk in obedience. While the tendency might be to "mostly" obey, I ask the Lord to help me obey fully. I don't want to miss anything He has for me. Also, being part of a community of believers is essential to walking in obedience. We need the encouragement, accountability, and prayers of our church community. Don't buy into the lie that you can tear down long-standing strongholds alone.

Bottom line: sometimes we try to take our thoughts captive to Jesus without first dealing with a central sin in our lives. That wall has to come down before we'll have the power to control our thinking.

> **PERSONAL RESPONSE:** *What recurring negative thoughts do you battle, even after having experienced real victory in a certain area? For instance, you may have experienced the tearing down of a stronghold of anger but you still struggle with thoughts of getting even or firing attacks you know you'd regret. Maybe the Lord toppled a stronghold of lying and dishonesty in your life, but occasionally your knee-jerk reaction is to shade the truth to accomplish your agenda. List two thoughts below and next to each one write what making them obedient to Christ would look like.*
>
> *Stray, defeating thought #1:*
>
>
> *Stray, defeating thought #2:*

AS WE CLOSE TODAY'S STUDY, REREAD VERSE 6.

Paul was patient, kind, compassionate, and zealous for the Corinthians. He loved them deeply, which is why he would not be afraid to deal with disobedience. But what had to happen before Paul would punish the disobedience of the false influencers?

I can't read this verse without thinking of one particularly precarious season of my life. The Lord and I were doing some serious siege warfare to a few strongholds. I was taking my thoughts captive to Jesus, even if sometimes it felt like trying to keep kittens in a box, as my assistant Bethany likes to say. They jumped out a lot. At one point, I remember wondering when God was going to deal with some of the people who had hurt me or focus on them for a while! And then I remember reading those words: *when your obedience is complete.* It was as if the Lord was saying to me, *Kelly, just keep doing what I've asked you to do. Keep thinking my thoughts. Keep obeying all the way until you've completed the task. I'll handle everyone else.*

PERSONAL RESPONSE: *We've covered a lot of ground today. We've gone to some deep places, and my prayer is that you're encouraged to take down walls in God's power. Since today was such a personal study, I'll leave the last question to you. How do you sense God wants you to respond today? Journal your thoughts below.*

DAY 4
A SOFT ANSWER

2 CORINTHIANS 10:1-2,7-11

One of Webster's definitions for the word *practical* is *suitable for everyday use.*[7] Despite the cultural differences, ancient practices, and original languages that can differ widely from English, I have never found a book more suitable for everyday use than the Word of God. Today we'll continue to explore the compassionate yet unbending ways in which Paul addresses those who didn't exactly care for him. You may be in a similar situation in your family or work environment where you're being unjustly accused or misunderstood. Today we'll look at how to respond in those situations.

I deliberately skipped over 2 Corinthians 10:1-2 yesterday because it connects well with verses 7-11, which we'll look at in today's study.

FIRST, READ 2 CORINTHIANS 10:1 IN THE MARGIN.

Paul was probably being facetious when he said he was "humble" when with them but "bold" when away. His detractors must have accused him of these things, a charge Paul kindly but strongly refuted.

With what two characteristics does Paul appeal to the Corinthians?

> Now I, Paul, make a personal appeal to you by the gentleness and graciousness of Christ—I who am humble among you in person but bold toward you when absent.
> 2 Corinthians 10:1, HCSB

These two words will set the tone for the last part of Paul's letter and our final weeks together. Gentleness and graciousness can deceptively seem like tame attributes, yet when their source is Christ, they can positively change our relationships when genuinely implemented. Let's look at them in the Greek. (Note: Your translations may use different English words, which is why we'll use the HCSB in the margin for consistency.)

The original Greek word for *gentleness* describes temperament of mind and heart, while the Greek word behind *graciousness* is more focused on the action of that inward disposition.[8] In other words, if gentleness is the car, graciousness is the car driving down the road.

Let's look first at *graciousness*. The Greek word for *graciousness* here is: *epieikeia*. It means *suitableness, equity, mildness—clemency (fairness).* One scholar, Matthew Arnold, describes *epieikeia* as, "sweet reasonableness."[9] Who isn't desperate for some reasonableness in our world right now?

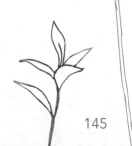

Sometimes I think I'd even take it unsweetened. The word can also mean *making allowances despite facts that might suggest reason for a different reaction.*[10]

I have a friend who is very measured in her responses. I wish I was more like her and not quite as fast to fly off the handle or feel the need to fix things the second they unravel. Part of this word *graciousness* means we don't have to implement the full use of our power or authority simply because we have it—Paul didn't want to bear down on the Corinthians if he didn't have to.

PERSONAL RESPONSE: *In what specific relationship in your life could you stand to be more gracious, measured, mild, or reasonable? Explain.*

Let's go back to the first word Paul used to describe the way in which he appealed to the Corinthians. The Greek word for *gentleness* is *praotēs*. It means *of a soothing disposition.*[11] But the word has a deeper meaning that is difficult to translate in English. We simply don't have an equivalent word. We tend to think of gentleness as meekness, which can sometimes be perceived as weakness. But that is not at all the case. In a sense, gentleness is great power under control. Jesus had the infinite resources of God at His command, yet He surrendered that power by walking in obedience to God. I'll sum it up this way: gentleness is power fully surrendered to God.

One of the best ways to understand a word in the Bible is to see how it's used in different passages. So let's look up a few verses that use the word *praotēs* and answer the corresponding questions. (Note: Many translations will use some form of the word *gentle*, but all have the Greek word *praotēs* behind them.)

READ GALATIANS 6:1.

Paul warns us to watch ourselves so we don't also fall into temptation. How does this awareness help us maintain a spirit of gentleness when we're correcting others?

READ 2 TIMOTHY 2:24-26.

How does having a patient and gentle spirit make you a better teacher? Really give this some thought.

READ 1 PETER 3:15-16.

In what specific context does Paul tell us to show gentleness?

Note that all of these verses deal with either correcting a struggling believer or sharing our hope with an unbeliever in the spirit of *praotēs*. In other words, this kind, humble, gracious, meek word is to be specifically used toward those who are lost or toward believers who are driving us a little bit nuts.

> **PERSONAL RESPONSE:** *Consider a current relationship you have with someone who doesn't know Christ or is a struggling believer. How could relating to them in meekness and gentleness make a difference in the relationship? What would that look like? Be specific.*

As I write today's study, I'm struggling with a lack of gentleness toward someone in my life. This person is stubborn, a bit manipulative, pretty selfish—I'm getting upset just writing about it. I'd like to tell you that if I just dig deep enough into my heart I'd eventually hit that stream of gentleness Paul is talking about. But look back at verse 1.

Where do gentleness and graciousness come from?

> **PERSONAL RESPONSE:** *Take a moment to ask the Lord to give you these Christ-like virtues. We will need Him to work these out in us, changing our hearts for the good as we share hope and confront difficulty.*

READ 2 CORINTHIANS 10:2.

Verse 2 can be interpreted in different ways. Some scholars interpret this verse to mean Paul's adversaries thought he was behaving in an unspiritual way. My impression is that his opponents were judging him by the world's standards. The Corinthian dissenters were looking for Paul to be a strong, philosophical orator who could command crowds. They probably expected that a true leader from God would be wealthy and have connections and resources. They were evaluating Paul by the reigning worldly values at the time. Regardless of your interpretation of 10:2, Paul was either being wrongly evaluated or falsely accused.

READ 2 CORINTHIANS 10:7-11.

According to verse 8, what is spiritual authority to be used for? What is it not to be used for?

PERSONAL REFLECTION: *All of us have spheres of authority. Whether you're a mother of young children, a business manager, teacher, or spiritual minister, we all have them. How have you used your authority in both the positive and negative ways Paul speaks of? What has been the result of both?*

Paul says that his authority was given by the Lord and was to be used for building up the Corinthians. Our spiritual authority is also given by God and should be used in the same way. I want this! I want to use my God-given authority with gentleness and graciousness for the good of others. How much more drawn to the church would the world be if all of us as believers used our spiritual authority, in whatever capacity we have it, for building other people up instead of tearing them down?

This does not mean that Paul—or any spiritual leaders for that matter—should be a pushover who never enforces any rules. Here's where the good tension of extending grace and applying discipline comes into play. We need the discernment of the Holy Spirit to know when to emphasize each.

According to verse 11 the tone of Paul's letters is no different than how he intends to be in person. He's not duplicitous. Unfortunately, sometimes I can put forth my best behavior when I want to impress someone I'm with, while not being as congenial when I'm with close friends or family.

I can only imagine what it must have been like for Paul to straddle the fence between grace and discipline. Not that the two are at odds, both are a means to lead us into a deeper relationship with Jesus. But it takes discernment to know when to implement them. My hope for you is this: if you struggle with being an authoritarian who bears down on others, my prayer is that you will learn to display graciousness and gentleness. And if you're continually being walked on and struggling to assert your God-given authority, my prayer is that you'll step up and lead with courage for the sake of building others up—even if that means you have to discipline or correct every once in a while.

As we grow in the likeness of Jesus may our gentleness be palatable, our graciousness filled with long-suffering, and our authority used for building others up.

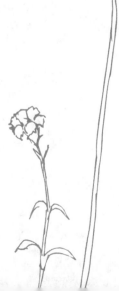

LIVING YOUR ASSIGNMENT

2 CORINTHIANS 10:12-18

In his sermons, my dad has often described the tendency we have as human beings to compare ourselves with one another. Whether we're picking up a baseball bat as a young child or trying on a dress for the high school prom, we intuitively assess the averages around us. Did I hit the ball farther than everyone or not as far as anyone? Is my dress size bigger or smaller than all the others girls going to the dance? How are my kids faring with the other children in the neighborhood? Whether we realize it or not, we're perpetually evaluating the average skill sets, appearances, smarts, abilities, and success rates of those around us. We want to know where we fit in this world and comparing ourselves amongst ourselves is one of the ways we try to find out. Hence, we often default to calculating the average successes of those around us.

Comparing ourselves against a standard isn't all bad. How would we know where to improve or when to be encouraged if we had no mark to strive toward? The trouble and danger come when the standard to which we aspire is based on worldly values—deeming ourselves successful when we hit that worldly standard or a failure when we fall short. As you begin today's Scripture reading, my prayer is that the Lord will use this text to free you from measuring sticks that keep you feeling smug or small. Paul will offer us a way of measuring ourselves apart from the world's way. We're in for a great day of study.

READ 2 CORINTHIANS 10:12-18.

Let's revisit our context for a moment. Paul was addressing the false apostles and opposing minority who had sought to undermine and discredit him. They'd judged and refuted his ministry by using a measuring rod forged by Corinthian values: wealth, speaking skills, influence, pride, and outward competence, among other things. To win at the comparison game, they had to excel by their own standards and knock anyone down they felt was gaining on them.

According to verse 12, how does Paul describe people who measure themselves by themselves and compare themselves with themselves?

What does Paul say he does not do?

Consider the subtle differences between measuring ourselves by ourselves and comparing ourselves with ourselves. I think of the former as trying to live up to whatever standards we perceive others are aiming for, and the latter as determining our success by how everyone else is doing at reaching those standards.

PERSONAL REFLECTION: *With which do you struggle most: Using the world's standards to define your achievements, or constantly comparing yourself with others to define your worth? Explain.*

In Paul's context, the problem wasn't comparison thinking per se, but the type of comparison-thinking that was taking place. I see three problems in particular.

1. The opposition had set a standard based on worldly values rather than righteousness.

2. The opposition used their faulty standards as a way of comparing themselves with one another.

3. The opposition found worth and identity in living up to their man-made standards and pride in doing it better than everyone else.

PERSONAL REFLECTION PART A: *What standard have you been trying to live up to that is based on worldly values rather than godly ones?*

PART B: *How do you hurt yourself and others when you measure success by how well you meet a worldly standard?*

You probably noticed that Paul used some form of the term *boast* several times in this passage. Answer the following questions for a deeper understanding of why.

Verses 13-15: True or False: Paul's boasting had limitations.

Verse 14: What allowed for Paul's boasting (the pride he had) in the Corinthians?

Verses 15-16: What did Paul refuse to brag about?

READ VERSE 13 IN THE HCSB IN THE MARGIN.

The phrase the HCSB renders "area of ministry" means *a portion measured off*. The Corinthians were part of God's assignment to Paul, an allotment God had measured off for Paul and his fellow laborers.

> We, however, will not boast beyond measure but according to the measure of the area of ministry that God has assigned to us, which reaches even to you.
> 2 Corinthians 10:13, HCSB

PERSONAL REFLECTION: *How does God calling you to certain people, places, and areas of ministry free you to live your ministry assignment without having to compare yourself to others?*

Most forms of comparison-thinking are detrimental, especially when used in spiritual settings. The enemy loves to sidetrack our ministries by tempting us to evaluate our giftings, callings, skill sets, personalities, and fields of ministry with those of other believers. The discouragement that comes from comparing ourselves among ourselves feels even more prominent since the advent of the Internet and social media. We can instantly look at other people's homes, families, children's activities, jobs, social statuses, and vacation excursions at the click of a button and wonder if what we do, where we live, and who we're raising has any meaning. And when we compare ourselves in this way, we will either feel unduly proud or unduly a failure.

PERSONAL TAKE: *Look back at verse 16. What areas did Paul make sure he didn't take credit for?*

> *Dear reader, when the Lord entrusts you with a ministry assignment, you will not only delight in it, you'll be able to rest in it.*

Paul's opponents were claiming Corinth as their area of ministry in a blatantly ungodly way. They were selfishly bragging about work Paul and his friends had labored for, and they were teaching false doctrine that was leading believers astray. Though Paul may not have had the swagger or public speaking chops the false apostles were championing, he had something infinitely grander—an assignment from God. Dear reader, when the Lord entrusts you with a ministry assignment, you will not only delight in it, you'll be able to rest in it. And if you're pining for someone else's assignment, relinquish that fight. You don't want to encroach on someone else's territory because God's given you your own. It will bring you neither joy nor satisfaction.

PERSONAL RESPONSE: *If you're jealous over someone else's calling or assignment, confess that struggle to the Lord by writing it below. Then, ask the Lord to reveal or confirm the assignment He has for you. And remember, this may change with different seasons.*

In verse 17, Paul quotes from Jeremiah 9:23-24. Contemplatively read this passage and fill in the blanks.

- *The wise man should not boast in his _____.*

- *The strong man should not boast in his_____.*

- *The wealthy man should not boast in his_____.*

Which of the three are you most likely to be proud about and why?

Jeremiah 9:24 thoroughly reveals who we can boast about and why. Write the verse below.

PERSONAL TAKE: *Why should we boast about a God who is personal, and who exercises kindness, justice, and righteousness on earth? (Remember in those days people believed in gods who were capricious, impersonal, and distant. Even today many believe in energy, a force, or the "universe" as a god.)*

Turn back to 2 Corinthians 10:18. Whom is the one God approves?

This is the key we've been longing for: when the Lord commends a person all other earthly comparisons and measuring rods are rendered irrelevant. Paul couldn't measure up to the false apostles' social standing, wealth, or worldly influence, nor did he aspire to. And he was unwilling to flaunt the areas he did excel in. The offending Corinthians could play their own game by their own rules with their own made-up goal posts, but Paul wasn't interested in jumping on that team. He was working for a Kingdom not of this world, whose King's approval is the only approval that matters. In John 5:44 Jesus said to the Pharisees, "How can you believe since you accept glory from one another but do not seek the glory that comes from the only God?"

When the Lord commends a person all other earthly comparisons and measuring rods are rendered irrelevant.

After spending much of my life seeking praise and approval from people, I have never enjoyed a deeper satisfaction than experiencing God's approval, sensing His commendation, and knowing He is pleased. The measuring rods of this world are fundamentally flawed, and they constantly fluctuate. I will continually be selfishly proud or disappointed if they become the standard by which I measure my worth or lack thereof. As believers, our lives are about God's glory and loving others, and this frees us from the comparison game.

As we close another week together, I can't tell you how inspired I am by your diligence in studying this deeply. You've tackled the personal and practical issues of sacrificial giving, tearing down strongholds, threading graciousness and gentleness into your relationships, embracing your God-given assignments, and confronting the pain of comparison thinking. You're so close to finishing 2 Corinthians and gaining a deep understanding of the letter in its entirety! Keep going—the last two weeks of study hold invaluable challenges and encouragement. This is a measuring rod worth reaching for.

SESSION 6 VIEWER GUIDE

A GOOD KIND OF BOASTING

GROUP DISCUSSION:

Paul appeals to the Corinthians in the meekness and gentleness of Christ. Is that how you appeal to the difficult people in your life? Explain.

How can we consistently display the attributes of meekness and gentleness?

How would you define a spiritual stronghold? If you're willing to share personally, give an example of a spiritual stronghold you've battled.

Do you ever struggle to complete your obedience? Explain. How does a small area of incomplete obedience equal total disobedience?

How does comparison thinking tempt us to live someone else's assignment? What's the downside of this? How can you keep your eyes fixed on what God has appointed you to do?

What one thing stood out to you from this video?

Before you label this dish as too frou-frou or healthy, just trust me on this one. While it is healthy, it's not granola-crunchy healthy. It's just tasty healthy. And if it happens to be summer, the seasonal cherry tomatoes, crisp cucumbers and fresh herbs make this dish amazing.

Hummus Chicken over Quinoa Salad (serves 4)

INGREDIENTS:	
1 lemon	6 sprigs mint, destemmed and chopped
1 cup quinoa (or bulgur wheat)	6 sprigs parsley, destemmed and chopped
¼ cup pine nuts	6 sprigs cilantro, destemmed and chopped
4 tablespoon olive oil, divided	6 ounces feta cheese
4 boneless, skinless chicken breasts	
Salt and pepper	
¾ cup hummus	
2 tablespoons sesame seeds	
2 medium-sized cucumbers, diced	
(peel first if desired)	
1 pint cherry tomatoes, halved	
6 green onions, thinly sliced	

DIRECTIONS
Preheat oven to 425 degrees.

Using a vegetable peeler, remove 5 long strips of zest from the lemon. Add zest and quinoa to a small pot and cook according to package directions.

Meanwhile, add pine nuts to a dry pan and toast over medium-high heat about 2 to 3 minutes, shaking occasionally to toss and being careful not to burn. Remove from pan and set aside.

Season chicken breasts with salt and pepper on both sides. In the same pan you used to toast pine nuts, heat 2 tablespoons olive oil. When oil is hot, add chicken breasts to pan and sear first side for 3 minutes without disturbing. Turn to sear second side for 3 minutes. Once flipped, use a spoon to spread hummus atop chicken, covering evenly. Sprinkle sesame seeds on hummus. Transfer chicken to a baking dish and place in preheated oven. Bake for 18 to 20 minutes, or until internal temperature reaches 165 degrees.

While chicken bakes, prepare cucumbers, cherry tomatoes, green onions, and herbs for the salad. Season the cherry tomatoes halves with salt. Toss all vegetables and herbs into a large serving bowl. Add pine nuts, quinoa, and feta cheese. Squeeze juice of half of the zested lemon over mixture. Drizzle remaining 2 tablespoons olive oil on top, and stir to combine. Salt and pepper to taste. Cut remaining half of lemon into wedges.

Divide salad mixture between 4 plates, and place 1 chicken breast on each salad. Serve with lemon wedges.

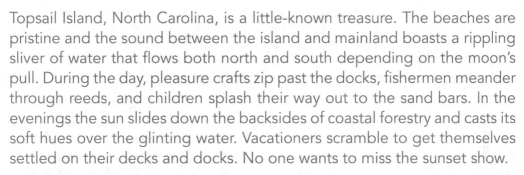

CHRIST'S POWER IN OUR WEAKNESS

Topsail Island, North Carolina, is a little-known treasure. The beaches are pristine and the sound between the island and mainland boasts a rippling sliver of water that flows both north and south depending on the moon's pull. During the day, pleasure crafts zip past the docks, fishermen meander through reeds, and children splash their way out to the sand bars. In the evenings the sun slides down the backsides of coastal forestry and casts its soft hues over the glinting water. Vacationers scramble to get themselves settled on their decks and docks. No one wants to miss the sunset show.

I was vacationing there with a few friends when one of them suggested we hop in the kayak and paddle our way across the sound to the mouth of an inlet that's lined with marshes. Small waterways serpentine through those marshes—wide enough for a kayak to pass through, long enough for a line to be cast. The fish were calling. Actually they weren't saying anything—they're kind of quiet that way. But we knew they were out there. The swaying reeds, the dive-bombing birds, a telling splash here and there. And I forgot to mention the clouds had blotted out what I'm almost certain were the words "Red Drum."

We grabbed our rods and oars, a bucket of live shrimp, a crunchy bag of frozen mullet, and off we rowed, perpendicular to the choppy current. We lurched in fits and splashes, mostly forward, because graceful kayakers we are not. After exactly 300 strokes, we'd made it to the other side and the keel slid up the bank of a sand bar. We lumbered out one at a time because we're no longer kids. (When you're a kid, you alight out of a kayak; when you're older, you lumber.) We gathered our rods, and April clamored for a shrimp out of the bucket. She pinched him between her fingers and pierced him through with my hook because you should

know at this point in the story that I don't like to bait my own hook. For one thing, shrimp are nasty little creatures with beaks. (You don't know this if your only exposure to them is at parties dipped in cocktail sauce. And don't get me started on that black vein.)

For an hour and a half, I stood knee-deep in the ripples, slinging my bait across the inlet's mouth like an outdoor magazine was there to do a story on my fishing prowess. Time and time again, I tipped the rod back while the shrimp dangled on the hook against the cobalt sky like a Popsicle™ on a stick. *What fish wouldn't want this?*, I mused. The perfectly weighted sinker carried the bait across the fluttering waters after I winged the rod forward. The line zinged. The bait dropped beneath the surface of the water. And nothing. Absolutely not anything of substance for 90 minutes other than one truly annoyed sunfish I reeled in. You should also know that I don't like to take my own fish off the hook. But never mind those details. The imaginary outdoor magazine thinks I'm a real talent.

After chalking up one sunfish, we determined to call it a day. We swapped our rods out of the kayak for a net roughly the size of a hammock. We wanted to capture a few mud minnows before

returning home to replenish our supply of live bait. We are efficient this way. We each grabbed one end of the net and strategically worked our way toward the sand bar. We cornered the mud minnows and any other unsuspecting creatures like pitifully tiny shrimp and crabs and with a brisk sweep we scooped them into our clutches. They flapped and scurried around in captivity. This was the most excitement we'd had all day.

If you've cracked your heart open to someone or something that is leading you astray, I implore you to run back to the Scriptures.

April cupped our winnings in the palms of her hands with the intent of dropping them in the bucket. But when we turned around to get the bucket, the strangest thing had happened. Our boat had vanished. My first thought was, *how in the world had someone stolen our kayak right out from underneath us?* We were the only ones ridiculous enough to be out here in the first place! Then I remembered this little known phenomenon people refer to as the tide. Apparently it had come in, and our kayak had gone out, just like that. Our heads darted in all directions scanning every possible waterway it could have floated down. I was panicking. I shot my gaze toward our house, which looked the size of a Monopoly piece across the waterway. It was way too far to swim. "I see it!" April shouted. "I'm going after it!" she exclaimed while charging waist deep into the current eventually succumbing to a full swim.

"This is a bad idea!" I yelled after her. "We need to call someone to get us!"

That's when April reminded me her phone was in the kayak. Right. In the time it took for us to exchange two sentences we could no longer see the boat, and I'd just spotted a stingray mosey past me, swinging its tail like it had never witnessed a more pathetic situation. I got the feeling that stinging me was beneath him.

April disappeared into the marsh while I waited for rescue. (Because if you're keeping track, I don't bait my hooks, unhook my fish, nor do I swim after lost kayaks. I am nothing but baggage, really.) After several unnerving minutes the tip of the kayak emerged from the reeds. April was safely inside rowing toward me. I realized at this point it would have been well within her rights to leave me out there with my 6-ounce sunfish. But she nosed toward me, and I climbed in the boat, and we paddled across the sound.

After the kayak debacle, my thoughts drifted to 2 Corinthians. Why? Well, because right now all my thoughts lead there, as if it were Rome. I considered how Paul pleads with the Corinthians to stay in the boat of the gospel, to resist wading out into the tantalizing tide of false teaching that so easily sweeps away one's "sincere and pure devotion to Christ" (2 Cor. 11:3). I thought about cunning and deceptive leaders presenting a Jesus to the church at Corinth who was no Jesus at all. As if in a clashing sea of currents, I could hear Paul bellowing from Macedonia for his beloved church to stay afloat in the only gospel that can save them. Abandoning that gospel for something that feels better in the moment or seems more culturally relevant would only prove to leave them stranded in the end.

As I now contemplate this section of Paul's letter, I'm reminded that the times haven't changed all that much. The tides that clamor for our beliefs and affections have never ceased being on the move. They continue to creep up on us almost imperceptibly until one day we turn our heads while out of the boat and everything we thought we knew is gone. But it doesn't have to be this way. As we begin this week, my prayer is that the Holy Spirit will help us tighten up our theology where it's gotten sloppy. If you've cracked your heart open to someone or something that is leading you astray, I implore you to run back to the Scripture. We'll be reassured by the steadfast truths of the Word, reminded that whatever the world promises us may flow in today, but it will flow out tomorrow. Only the Jesus Paul preached will prove buoyant enough to hold us.

DAY 1
PURE JEALOUSY

2 CORINTHIANS 11:1-6

Whenever I see a doctor, especially for anything that could be linked to stress or tension, I try to present myself as a relaxed and cheery human. I think most doctors peg me wrong—they claim I'm intense. Recently I had an elongated visit with my doctor, and he emphatically told me some of the troubles I was having had to do with stress. *Me? You really think so, doctor?* Because you wouldn't believe how relaxed I was in his office—I was almost dead.

After my appointment, I trotted out into the lobby and spoke to the receptionist. She's a friend of mine who works for my doctor. "Tammi," I whispered, all collected. "He said he thinks I'm intense!" She feigned wonderment. "But you wouldn't believe how breezy I was! I was so breezy, like breezier than a swan skimming across the glassy waters of the sea."

"He's really good at studying people," Tammi said, while ringing me up. She handed me a bag of natural supplements that are derived from super foods. I told her I couldn't wait for everyone to see how easygoing I was about to be.

I don't know if Paul would have described himself as passionate, intense, or given to stress. He may have fought his intensity as I occasionally do. No one ever called Paul laid-back. In this week's study, Paul's passion and zeal crest to new heights out of love for the Corinthians and for the true gospel he preached to them. I'm thinking Paul could have benefited from the calming enzymes of certain super foods to deal with certain super apostles, but I don't know if he could get those kinds of supplements in Corinth. Plus, I'm thinking that if ever there was something to be ratchetted up about, it's people's souls. It's the gospel. It's Jesus Christ! So let's get ready to engage in some important material this week. I have no doubt we will see our own cultures and communities represented in chapter 11, becoming more clearly aware of the things that truly deserve our passion.

READ 2 CORINTHIANS 11:1-6.

What word does Paul use to describe his feelings for the Corinthians in verse 2?

Look back at Exodus 20:1-5. What similarity do you notice between God's passion for the Israelites and Paul's passion for the Corinthians?

Here's a definition for *jealousy: a strong feeling of possessiveness, often caused by the possibility that something which belongs, or ought to belong, to one is about to be taken away.* The word can be used in a positive sense (e.g. the jealousy of God), meaning a passionate commitment to something that rightly belongs to one. It can also be used in a negative sense (e.g. human jealousy) to mean a self-destructive human emotion similar to envy.[1]

We often think first of jealousy with negative connotations. I hate the feeling of being captive to jealousy's consuming nature that often leads to reckless and harmful actions. But there's a difference between being jealous of someone and being jealous for someone. And there's a difference between jealousy that finds its source in our flesh versus the Spirit.

Review today's passage and explain in detail why Paul was jealous for the Corinthians.

Paul also describes his jealousy as what?
- ❏ *consuming*
- ❏ *godly*
- ❏ *overpowering*
- ❏ *selfish*

I wouldn't want to serve a passive God any more than I would want to be married to a passive husband who didn't care where I was or who I was with. In the purest sense of the word, we cannot be jealous for another person if we don't first care for that person. Paul deeply cherished the Corinthians, which is why he was jealous for them. It's a strange sentiment to write, but I want to be more jealous. Jealous for the lost. Jealous for my friends, family, and the people I minister to to know Jesus more deeply. We simply won't have the energy for godly jealousy if we don't care about another person's spiritual condition.

If you're trying to decipher if the jealousy you're experiencing is godly or from your flesh, consider these questions:

Is your ultimate goal for the person to love Jesus with an undivided heart or to be attached to you?

Are you trying to control this person for your own purposes or liberate him/her?

Are you consumed by what you want this person to do for you, or how desperately you want him/her in relationship with Christ?

Do you see the differences here? Thinking through these questions will help you know what needs to be purified in your heart.

Read Ephesians 5:25-27, along with 2 Corinthians 11:2. Explain the significance of Paul describing the church's relationship to Christ as being like a sacred marriage between a husband and wife. How does this relate to the idea of godly jealousy?

Just as the marriage union is an exclusive and set-apart relationship, so our loyalty to Jesus should be pure and undivided. Since Paul had personally brought the gospel to the Corinthians, he considered himself their spiritual father. His deepest desire was to present them to Christ as a beautiful, pure bridegroom like a father would present his daughter to her husband. The problem is that the Corinthians were claiming a false Jesus along with other conflicting beliefs and false teachings. The church at Corinth was like a bride betrothed to her future husband while being involved with a bunch of other men. Let's look further into what was compromising the Corinthians' pure relationship to Jesus.

Verse 4 is the key to understanding the heart of the problem in the church of Corinth. What three distortions does Paul point out?

1.

2.

3.

According to verse 3 what did Paul fear? (Fill in the blank) The Corinthians'
_____ would be led astray.

To what biblical account did Paul compare the Corinthians' situation in verse 3, and with what adjective is the serpent described?

I want to consider the progression here. First of all, the battle starts with the mind. Just as the serpent in the garden challenged Eve's thinking, so the false teachers in Corinth were going after the believers' minds. They were challenging their Christ-centered thinking, beliefs, and world views. And they were doing so with a slick and convincing tongue that was wooing the Corinthians away from the true Jesus, His Spirit, and the pure gospel.

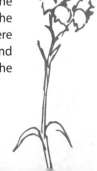

Paul warned that just as Eve was deceived by the serpent, we too can be deceived. But if being deceived means to be tricked or misled, how can we know when it's happening to us? Last night I talked to a family member who was describing how oppressed he'd felt a few days before. A lot of difficult trials and tragedies were surrounding him, and he found himself mentally sinking in a sea of swirling shadows. When I asked him how he pulled out of the despair, he simply said, "I knew what I needed to do. Go to the Scriptures." This will always be one of the chief protections for our minds from the deceptions of the enemy. If we're toying with or buying into a way of thinking that is contrary to God's Word, we're on the road to deception. If what we're beginning to believe doesn't match up with God's Word, we can know we're being deceived. So in a sense, we don't know when we're being deceived unless we let the Word of God tell us.

If we're toying with or buying into a way of thinking that is contrary to God's Word, we're on the road to deception.

> *Look back at verse 4. We know the false teachers were preaching a different Jesus than the true Christ Paul had preached to them. This led to some of the Corinthians having _____ a different spirit and gospel.*

Things become really dangerous when we receive contrary thoughts and beliefs into our thinking and eventually into our hearts. Paul says at the end of verse 4 that the Corinthians had no problem with the detractors teaching a different Jesus. They received it without being troubled in any way. You, too, may be struggling with a once-tightly held biblical belief you are no longer sure is true because of what you've recently read, watched, or experienced. Go back to the Word and find the truth.

PERSONAL RESPONSE: *Ask the Lord to show you if you have received as truth a compromised version of Christ or His gospel. If so, repent and turn back to the real truth.*

When the enemy comes to deceive us he does so cunningly. Remember, the serpent in the garden of Eden was cursed to crawl on his belly after Eve ate of the tree. There's no telling how charming he may have looked, or with what swagger he strutted into the garden before twisting the logic of God's Word. He must have seemed believable, his arguments buyable, and his promises desirable for Eve to have been deceived. This is why we must continually immerse ourselves in the Word. When the tantalizing winds of culture's "liberating arguments" blow through our thoughts, we can then protect ourselves from being lulled into deception by countering false wisdom with biblical truth.

Paul couldn't bear to see the false teachers in Corinth lead his new converts astray. But notice he didn't fear the Corinthians being led astray from religion, a denomination, or even from his own self. He was afraid they'd be led away from their pure devotion to Christ! This is what allowed Paul's jealousy to fall underneath the godly category. His sole passion was to present the Corinthians purely to Jesus as a father would give his daughter as a bride to her bridegroom. As we start the this week, I'm jealous for you to know the difference between the world's cunning teaching and the wisdom of Jesus. I'm jealous for you to see the thinness of materialism against the adventure of a Christ-following life. I'm jealous for you to experience the satisfying love of Jesus, sold out for no other. This is pure jealousy.

WHAT MATTERS MOST

2 Corinthians 11:5-15

Our culture places a premium on beauty, talent, skill level, wealth, social status, charisma, people skills, and fame. Paul's Corinth was no different. Even in the church today we gravitate to the successful over those we deem common. How many times have you thought, *how awesome a Christian would a specific movie star or famous athlete or wealthy business owner be?* But we may not have that same thought about the widow at the end of our street or the troubled middle class family in our neighborhood. This is not to say that any of the aforementioned accolades are inherently sinful or shouldn't be pursued with the right heart. The problem comes when outward appearance and social standing are what we use to evaluate spiritual worth or success—our own or someone else's.

The church at Corinth had stumbled into that very trap, buying into the teachings and claims of the false apostles simply because these men were persuasive, charismatic, and influential. Paul had quite an impressive list of accomplishments to his name as well, but either the Corinthians didn't value those achievements, or Paul chose to withhold some of them so as not to take away from the pure power of the gospel. This will become clearer as we begin today's study.

READ 2 CORINTHIANS 11:5-15.

According to verse 6, what skill(s) does it seem Paul was lacking, according to the Corinthians?

What can we surmise they were accusing him of in verses 7-9?
❏ *Charging an expensive honorarium*
❏ *Preaching for free*
❏ *Stealing to support himself*

List all the ways Paul humbled himself so as not to be a burden to the Corinthians.

Paul couldn't win with the Corinthians. If he'd charged them a fortune to minister in their church they would have called him a charlatan; when he didn't charge them at all, they were offended. Most speakers in ancient Corinth were paid professionals and those who came to listen expected to pay, hoping part of their money could purchase them closeness to the speaker. If Paul had allowed the Corinthians to support him financially they may have tried to use it as leverage to control him or his message. Also, Paul's manual labor as a tentmaker was an embarrassment to them. "An impoverished leader was a contradiction in terms."[2] Even though Paul was bringing the life-changing message of Jesus, he wasn't sharing it the way they wanted. We're getting an idea of how political ministry had become in Corinth. Still, Paul refused to change from a humble approach to a conceited one. Oddly enough, his humble service is something he'll actually boast about.

Review verse 11. What reason does Paul give for why he chose to humbly serve the Corinthians?

The Corinthians would have been happier with Paul if he had served and loved them according to their specific ideas and conditions. They wanted Paul to rely on their pay so he could be subject to them. They desired that he fit into their social norms by dropping the lowly tent-making gig and jumping on the speaking circuit. The problem is that all of this would have undermined Paul's pure love for them. To minister under the constructs of the Corinthian culture was really no ministry at all.

PERSONAL REFLECTION: *Have you ever felt pressure to change your ministry approach or the way you showed love to someone based solely on what that person wanted? Explain. If you compromised a genuine approach, what was the result?*

To get a better picture of the flashy Corinthian approach versus Paul's humble service, turn back to 1 Corinthians 2:1-5.

Fill in the columns below:

The Way Paul Ministered	The Way Paul Didn't Minister

Paul may not have preached with the ornamental and haughty speaking skills the Corinthians were accustomed to, but what accompanied his speaking according to verse 4?

According to verse 5, why would Paul rather preach in weakness than out of his intellectual prowess?

CONTINUE READING 1 CORINTHIANS 2:5-7,10

What word is used several times to characterize Paul's message?

❏ *intellect*   ❏ *charisma*

❏ *charm*   ❏ *wisdom*

How do we get wisdom (v. 10)?

Paul isn't saying we shouldn't work hard at our crafts or refine our skills and talents. He's also not promoting laziness that leans on the convenient excuse that the Spirit will somehow take care of our unpreparedness. (I've tried to fall back on this one a time or two.) In context, the Corinthian false teachers were attempting to dissuade people from the true gospel by their sharp oratory skills and intellectualism. Paul pointed out that human pride and smarts are no match for God's wisdom and power. Whether we are skilled or unskilled, educated or uneducated, the power of the gospel shines through humble vessels.

As I write this, I'm in the midst of preparing to lead worship at an event for ministry leaders. I could list countless people who have broader singing ranges and silkier voices with guitar skills that pick circles around my strumming. I'm working hard, but I'm limited in my abilities. When I look at a passage like this, I'm encouraged that even in my shortcomings I can pray and trust that the power of God's anointing will rest upon me as I lead worship.

Turn back to 2 Corinthians 11:6. Instead of being a trained speaker, what did Paul say he had?

Let's put this together because it has profound meaning. Dear reader, we live in a world where people don't know where they're going. They don't know what to hope in or if hope even exists. Many don't know why they're here. They're chasing every imaginable dream to no avail. For a season, they may have woken up for a certain pleasure until one day that pleasure stopped satisfying or it walked out the door. But you and I don't live with that emptiness. We have the knowledge and wisdom Paul wrote about because God has revealed it to us by His Spirit (1 Cor. 2:10). And the knowledge He revealed is "the knowledge of God's glory in the face of Jesus Christ" (2 Cor. 4:6, HCSB). And we carry this treasure in jars of clay, not refined, showy vessels (2 Cor. 4:7).

The wisdom and knowledge of Jesus is what the world is desperate for. We don't have to be an expert in the latest trends, or have razor-sharp skills designed to buy people's respect, impress them with our beauty, or make them covet our positions. The world has all this in spades! It doesn't need more of its own stuff. What people are longing for is to meet someone with abiding spiritual wisdom and knowledge about what truly matters. Someone to tell them the secret wisdom of God that rescues us from loneliness, satiates our longings, obliterates the strongholds that keeps us addicted, and washes our consciences clean!

Plain and simple, this secret wisdom is cultivated by time in God's Word. It's quickened in prayer. It's deepened by fellowship with other believers. It's revealed in greater degrees when we're obedient. You can't buy the secret things of God, but He's pleased to give them to the ones who seek Him.

DAY 3
A FOOLISH BOAST

2 CORINTHIANS 11:16-30

Today's passage is an interesting one to say the least. It's not often we read the apostle Paul admit he's not speaking as the Lord would, or according to God's ways. This doesn't mean Paul was out from underneath God's authority; it means he's taken his Christianity off-roading into the woods after the Corinthians because he's tried everything else to convince them of his apostleship. If he can't beat his opponents, he's going to momentarily join them in their tactics, but not to achieve their goals—that's the key difference. Paul will stoop to the bragging shenanigans of the false teachers only to ultimately prove his undying love and commitment to the church at Corinth, and to turn everyone's sights back to Jesus. If you've ever thought Christianity is simply a matter of following a list of rules, today will prove it's far more relational and creative than that. Not to mention adventurous.

READ 2 CORINTHIANS 11:16-30.

Paul's situation is reminiscent of challenges we face today. Charming, charismatic personalities who claim to love God and may even claim to follow Jesus are leading countless believers down paths that are at odds with God's Word. The Corinthian church was filled with new believers who were especially vulnerable to the pull of the super apostles. These false teachers claimed to be God's leaders, but were actually about their own position and power. Paul had no choice but to go head-to-head with them for the sake of the church he loved.

Paul's opponents were bragging according to human standards, swaying the church away from Paul and ultimately Christ. In verse 18 and 21b Paul says he too is going to start boasting. What types of things did he boast about according to the rest of the passage?

According to verse 30, how did Paul describe what he boasted about? Why do you think he boasted about these things?

The Lord has used today's passage to convict me. Honestly, I like to stay out of the fray. I'm not one to jump into controversy. I fear people twisting my words, I hate being misunderstood, and I generally dislike being disliked. (Did you notice my fears are all about me?) Pretty much all the controversy that swirls around taking a stand is everything I try to avoid. In other words, no one has to worry about me ever running for president. We are in a battle, though, and the Lord has not called us to live our lives shirking from uncomfortable situations. If the world is going to use its megaphone to cast its sway over the people we're called to be ministers of reconciliation to, how much more should you and I boast about who Jesus is and what He's done in our lives?

> **PERSONAL REFLECTION:** *Consider the way people who are not believers (or confused believers) flaunt and promote their false beliefs. How can you graciously but boldly boast about Jesus and what He's done in your life? If this is difficult for you, list what stands in your way.*

Review verse 20. Keep in mind Paul is not referring to a hypothetical situation but a real one that is affecting the church in Corinth. List the five harmful actions the church was putting up with from the false teachers. "You even put up with anyone who …"

1.

2.

3.

4.

5.

When I read this list I think, *why in the world would anyone put up with this?* I realize we can't know for sure, but I have to believe that if the Corinthian believers were taking this much abuse from the false teachers, something tantalizing was also being offered. I can't imagine they would have subjected themselves to this harsh treatment if they weren't being persuasively influenced, promised something desirable, or involved in some sort of codependent relationship with the false leaders. Remember, these enemies were masquerading as apostles of Christ and servants of righteousness—they weren't blatantly evil in appearance, rather they were Jesus-ish in persuasion (2 Cor. 11:13-15). I tend to forget this.

I personally experienced something similar at an impressionable time in my life. I desperately wanted to be on the inside with some dynamic personalities who were "spiritual" but not Christlike. I put up with all kinds of nonsense, never knowing when I was going to be chosen or left out. I allowed myself to be lied to and taken advantage of. After awhile I even let myself become deceived, all because I wanted acceptance. I truly praise God that I had a few people like Paul step into my life. They reminded me of what healthy, godly friendships look like in comparison to the misery I was experiencing.

PERSONAL TAKE: *Can you relate to this experience? If so, how? Add any insights the Holy Spirit is revealing to you about why you've allowed yourself to be hurt or taken advantage of.*

In a tongue-in-cheek sort of way, Paul says in verse 21 he was too weak for the kind of harsh treatment the false leaders displayed. Based on your study of 2 Corinthians so far, how was Paul's approach to ministry with the Corinthians different than the false teachers? What Christlike characteristics did Paul display?

If you're wondering if someone is a true servant of the Lord, ask yourself these questions: Is the person humble or proud? Gentle or harsh? Patient or explosive? A bragger of self-made accomplishments or a boaster of weaknesses that makes much of Jesus' strength?

Verses 22-29 are what many refer to as "The Fool's Speech" since Paul was put in a position to have to act foolishly by boasting about his spiritual experiences. As my friend Julie put it, "Paul didn't mention his humble service earlier because he was busy just doing it. Now they had forced him to come out and say what before he was just trying to show with his choices, his life, his work, his words."

What descriptions of identity and heritage does Paul begin with in verse 22? Why start here with his boasting?

Consider the physical hardships listed in verses 23-27 that Paul endured for the sake of the gospel. What convicts and challenges you the most and why?

For better understanding, I've paraphrased verses 28-29 below:

Apart from other things I could mention, I face daily the pressure of my concern for all the churches. Who is weak and I am not weak? Who is led into sin and I am not livid about it?[3]

PERSONAL TAKE: *Verses 28-29 shift from Paul's physical hardships and suffering to a more relational and emotional nature of suffering. Explain how relational pain—such as watching people you love be led astray—can be even more painful than physical suffering?*

When I look at the whole of Paul's speech, I'm challenged. He has leveraged his heritage, experiences, trials, and open heart to defend himself before the church he served. The persuasive personalities who looked like Christ's ministers and who were holding power over the Corinthian believers needed someone to stand up to them. We need people willing to take a stand for truth today. We're desperate for people to rise up with humility for the sake of others so Jesus can receive glory. If we fling ourselves out there with any other motives—even if we speak truth—we will be as foolish as the ancient false teachers.

If you consider yourself too weak or powerless to make any kind of difference, read Revelation 12:10-11 in the margin as an encouraging reminder. What does your testimony, in conjunction with the blood of the Lamb, have the power to do?

PERSONAL RESPONSE: *Don't rush to finish today. Take a moment to prayerfully journal about one specific way you can step up and take a necessary stand. (I'm praying the same.)*

Then I heard a loud voice in heaven say: The salvation and the power and the kingdom of our God and the authority of His Messiah have now come, because the accuser of our brothers has been thrown out: the one who accuses them before our God day and night. They conquered him by the blood of the Lamb and by the word of their testimony, for they did not love their lives in the face of death.
Revelation 12:10-11, HCSB

CAUGHT UP
TO HEAVEN

2 CORINTHIANS 11:30-33; 12:1-6

First, let me begin by saying I'm so proud of you! Not many people get this far into a Bible study. The chores of life creep in, enthusiasm wanes, and friends drop out. Then you're left with that awkward task of going to your group meeting alone, when all you really want is to be home on your couch with a bowl of cheese dip. I understand this. I want you to know that the cheese dip will come and go, but your time in the Word of God will never be taken from you. When Mary of Bethany sat at Jesus' feet as Martha prepared the meal, Jesus said that Mary's investment of time with Him would never be taken from her (Luke 10:42). Be encouraged. The time you're spending with the Lord is an eternal investment.

As I applaud your impressive discipline and commitment, according to today's text, I should be cheering you on for your weaknesses as well. Paul is going to show us yet again that we can take great joy in our frailties—not for frailties' sake, but because the power of Christ shines magnificently through our weakness.

READ 2 CORINTHIANS 11:30-33.

PERSONAL TAKE: *Write verse 30 in the margin. Then consider this question: Given the circumstances he faced with the Corinthian church, including the conflict with the "super apostles," why would Paul choose to boast about his weaknesses instead of his strengths?*

Were you perplexed by Paul inserting his account of being lowered in a basket from a window in the wall of Damascus? At first this struck me as an odd story in an odd place. I tucked it away as The Great Basket Mystery. (I have a large folder in my head for similar Bible questions.) Thankfully there is supplemental information in Acts that will shed further light. Before reading that text, keep in mind Paul's prestigious heritage and upbringing as a Jew of Jews. Also note the great basket escape happened soon after his salvation experience on the road to Damascus.

READ ACTS 9:9-15,22-25.

Paul had gone from being renowned in the Jewish community as a Pharisee intent on stomping out this movement called the Way (Acts 9:1-2), to a man on the run as a follower of its founder, Jesus. Explain how going from being a powerful leader to a fugitive fleeing for his life in a basket would be considered a weakness Paul could boast about.

We can all take a page out of Paul's evangelism and discipleship playbook here. Sharing what God has done in our marriages, friendships, child-raising, jobs, health, etc.—especially during times of weakness and vulnerability— is one of the most relatable ways to share our faith.

PERSONAL REFLECTION: *Can you think of an especially weak time in your life when Jesus showed Himself strong in your powerlessness? Describe how you can share this experience with believers and unbelievers alike in a way that makes the hope of Jesus accessible and relatable.*

A dear older friend of mine shared this story with me: "I remember a man coming in to service the cable. He said, 'Lady, is your house always this clean?' I told him I used to be a real pig! 'What happened to change you?' he asked. 'The Lord Jesus Christ!' I replied. I never expected to share about Jesus that day in that way. It is always exhilarating! I have grown to absolutely love the simple and unglamorous ways God can use us! It speaks more of His greatness to me that He cares about such little details."

TURN BACK TO 2 CORINTHIANS 12:1-6.

What heaven was Paul caught up to?
❑ *first*
❑ *second*
❑ *third*
❑ *fourth*

How many years prior to Paul's writing this letter had this experience happened?

According to verse 4, what types of things did Paul hear?

Why did Paul speak about himself in the third person? Some scholars suggest he didn't want to come off as arrogant about this extraordinary experience, so he used this grammatical tool to humbly detract attention from himself. Sharing about the amazing works God has done in our lives is vital for us to do, but we should be careful not to slip into a "bragimony." (One of my favorite made-up Christian terms for when a testimony turns into bragging about how awesome we are.)

When sharing about God's goodness in your life, what's one specific thing you can do to make sure God is the one being celebrated instead of exalting yourself? It can be something as simple as Paul using the third person to talk about his experience—except maybe don't imitate him exactly. That could be a little weird.

While several theories abound concerning "the third heaven," many scholars say Paul is referring to the highest heavenly realm, God's throne room. In verse 4 Paul calls it paradise. "It may be, therefore, that Paul was taken into the very presence of God in the heavenly holy of holies."[4] Paul's experience fits well with the obsession our modern culture—even secular culture—has with the afterlife and spirituality. Granted, much of what we watch on television or in movies about the spiritual realm is fictional or completely false. However, this fascination with it tells me that inherently we know we're more than physical beings existing only for this fading earth.

Why do you think Paul felt the need to share this experience with the Corinthians now after keeping it private for fourteen years?

Paul wasn't sure if his heavenly experience took place in the body or out of the body. It's possible he was confronting the gnostic belief prevalent at the time that the body was inherently evil, and therefore a truly divine experience couldn't have happened while in the body. Regardless, Paul was comfortable with whichever way the Lord had chosen to snatch him up. What I find meaningful is that both times Paul claimed to not know the answer to this mystery, he insisted, but "God knows" (vv. 2,3).

> **PERSONAL REFLECTION:** *Is there something in your life you've been spending precious energy trying to solve or figure out? If there doesn't appear to be a clear answer this side of heaven—or at least in the foreseeable future—take a moment to entrust it to the God who knows. Lay it before the One to whom no mysteries exist. Write your prayer below.*

Look back at the end of verse 6. What two things did Paul want to be noted for?

This is one of those enormously practical verses I'd skimmed over my whole life until now. After Paul relayed one of the most sacred, holy, and extraordinary experiences a person could ever have, he essentially said, *But enough about all that. The real reason I want you to trust my apostleship is because of the way I've lived my life before you. By what I do and say.* We love the sensational. We get excited for a miracle or a good vision or dream. Perhaps even more so today we're infatuated with the platforms of Christian celebrities, focusing on their big ministries—impressed more with size rather than effectiveness. But do we have the same level of passion for daily faithfulness? The humble service no one sees? The patient and kind word spoken in mundane conversations? Supernatural and extra-special experiences are wonderful, but it's the consistent godly patterns of our lives that yield enduring fruit.

Supernatural and extra-special experiences are wonderful, but it's the consistent godly patterns of our lives that yield enduring fruit.

> **PERSONAL REFLECTION:** *When you think about your life as a believer, what do you most seek: electrically-charged highs and supernatural experiences or daily faithfulness that's characterized by love, peace, patience, kindness, service, and joy? Explain.*

The Lord snatching a person up for anything—especially a visit to heaven—is an unspeakable privilege and blessing. I've had a few experiences in my life I would categorize as extraordinarily sacred or holy. At times, the Lord has spoken to my heart more clearly than if I'd heard Him audibly. He's given me experiences I would say were divine. I treasure these, and occasionally I share about them. You may have some, too. But at the end of our lives these mountain-top experiences will not be what we're remembered for. By God's grace, we will be a part of changing lives on this earth because of what we've said and done. Because of how we've humbly, sacrificially, and all-out joyfully lived our lives with day-to-day faithfulness.

Our culture makes much of the spotlight and the sensational. We even fall into this trap in the church sometimes. The bright lights will fade and the stage will one day have someone else dance across its surface. But those who do the will of the Lord will live forever (1 John 2:17). And His will is to love Him and love others. Let's do this in word and deed.

DAY 5
WHEN I'M WEAK, I'M STRONG

2 CORINTHIANS 12:7-10

When I'm weak I am strong

Suffering brings Your grace along

My deepest hurt becomes my greatest song

For when I'm weak I am strong

I wrote these words and put them to a simple melody when I was in college. I never got around to writing verses or a bridge or anything that would make this lyric into an actual song. It was my little chorus I strummed on my guitar, sometimes singing through tears. I was always a pretty serious kid—that one of my favorite passages of Scripture growing up was about Paul's thorn in the flesh, and that I wrote a chorus about it, is a testament to this. (My poor parents!) This is still one of the most meaningful passages in the Bible to me. Not so much because I love the idea of having a thorn, but because of the presence of Jesus who presses in deeper than the thorn. I'm praying you'll be encouraged by today's reading.

READ 2 CORINTHIANS 12:7-10.

The Greek word for *thorn* is *skolops* and can refer to "something sharp or pointed, such as a splinter or a stake."[5] Paul used this metaphor to speak of a particular pain that was difficult and unceasing. He also tells us the thorn was inherently evil, calling it "a messenger of Satan" (v. 7). I will speak more about this in this week's video, but let's look at the why, what, and who of the thorn. Answering these questions may be difficult and troubling at times, but once we do the hard work we'll be blessed by ending this week's study with the promise of Christ's power and presence in our lives, no matter what the thorn.

WHY THE THORN WAS GIVEN

Why was the thorn given (v. 7)?

PERSONAL TAKE: *Why would Paul becoming proud or conceited be one of the worst things that could happen to him, his ministry, and his relationship with the Lord?*

Of the why, what, and who of Paul's thorn in the flesh, the why is most clearly answered. As a result of Paul's supernatural experience with the Lord he would need this thorn to keep him walking in humility. We may not have all the information we'd like but let's give it up for at least one clear answer!

WHAT THE THORN WAS

Several ideas and opinions have been offered over the years as to the nature of Paul's thorn, but the reality is we simply don't know. Some believe it was a physical ailment; others believe it was persecution and continuing opposition; still a few think it was psychological travail. You can make arguments for any of these; however, a physical condition and persecution of some sort are the two with the most traction.

PERSONAL TAKE: *What benefit do we receive from not knowing the identity of Paul's thorn?*

We don't need to have Paul's thorn to experience the grace and power of Jesus; we only need to have a thorn.

In one way I'd love to know what Paul's thorn in the flesh was. Reading his letters with that knowledge in mind would give us more personalized insight into some of his writings. At the same time, I'm glad we don't know. That makes this passage more broadly applicable to any of us who have a thorn. We don't need to have Paul's thorn to experience the grace and power of Jesus; we only need to have a thorn. Lacking the thorn's specific identity, we focus on Jesus during our suffering rather than comparing our thorn to the nature of Paul's. If our thorn matched Paul's, consider how that one form of suffering would be exalted above every other form. Can you imagine? Just think of all the people who would be incessantly talking about their PTSD—Paul's Thorn & Suffering Disease. I think the Lord saved us big by not revealing this one.

THE WHO BEHIND THE THORN

According to verse 7, the thorn was _____ Paul.
❏ *received by*   ❏ *forced upon*
❏ *resisted by*   ❏ *given to*

The difficulty of this verse is that it's not crystal clear who the giver is—God or Satan. However, we do know that "The word *given* was usually employed to denote that God's favor had been bestowed."[6] We also know that God chose to not remove it and that He had a good purpose for the thorn. My personal belief—and the view of scholars I've studied—is that God was the giver of the thorn. I know this can be difficult to accept—it's hard for me to accept—especially since we know the thorn was evil. But regardless of whether you view God or Satan as the giver, tension exists. Either God gave the thorn, which has its obvious difficulties, or Satan gave it while God stood by and allowed it. Either way we're left to contend with God about a difficult matter.

> **PERSONAL REFLECTION:** *What in verse 7 causes you the most difficulty with God? If no difficulty exists for you, explain.*

We're not the first people to struggle with the question, *if God is good how could He give an evil thorn or permit pain He could have stopped?* We also see this play out in John 11. Mary and Martha's brother Lazarus was deathly ill. They sent for Jesus while their brother was still alive, pleading for Jesus to come and heal him. But Jesus didn't come in time (11:6).

READ JOHN 11:33-37.

Mary and Martha's Jewish friends had two very different responses when they saw Jesus weeping alongside Mary. What were they?

What was the chief complaint about Jesus from the second group?

The other day I took one of those walks with the Lord where I prayed and praised, but also contended. I confessed to the Lord that one of the greatest challenges to my faith is seeing the lost dying without the gospel. Also, it's very difficult for me to watch tragedies fall on believers and unbelievers alike that God has the power to stop. If He knew the trajectory of this decaying world and our wicked hearts, why start this whole thing in the first place? I was hashing these questions out with the Lord on my walk—not expecting an answer but more interested in receiving a deeper assurance of His great love for the world.

A few hours later, I was thumbing through the passage you just read, preparing for a message I was giving to a group of women. I've read John 11 bunches of times, but had never noticed the significance of the two distinct responses to the exact same event. Both groups witnessed Jesus weeping with Mary near Lazarus's tomb. One group's eyes were opened to Jesus' profound love for Lazarus—*See how He loved him!* But the other group was filled with a sea of doubt—*If He has the power to heal, why didn't He?* The first group was focused on what Jesus had done; the second on what He could have done but didn't.

> **PERSONAL REFLECTION:** *When it comes to the troubles and difficulties of life, how can you more purposely focus on what Jesus has done for you versus what He hasn't?*

TURN BACK TO 2 CORINTHIANS 12:8.

True or False: Paul received the thorn without objection.

What helps buoy me through the difficulties of verses 7-8 are verses 9-10. After Paul pleaded with the Lord three times to remove the thorn, what was Jesus' personal response to him? Write the quote in verse 9.

Regardless of the type of thorns we've been given or hardships we're enduring I'm a big believer in pleading with the Lord. I encourage you to beg the Lord for healing, deliverance, and relief. Scripture backs up our persistent appeal to God for help in times of trouble. However, there are times when the Lord tells us to move forward with our thorns. If He chooses to keep the difficulty in place, we must choose to live in the promises of verses 9-10. It's a willful decision we must make. I've spent way too much time sidelined by certain pain, trying to dissect it and figure it out, instead of experiencing Christ's sufficient grace and perfect power in the midst of it.

> **PERSONAL REFLECTION:** *In the midst of your most painful trial, how has Jesus' grace been sufficient for you?*

How has His power been made complete in your weakness?

After Paul hears from Jesus his tone significantly changes. He goes from pleading with the Lord to remove the thorn to what entirely new response?

The thorn had not changed but Paul's perspective had. Instead of solely seeing the evil of the thorn and focusing on the pain of it, he realized it was an avenue through which Christ's power could rest upon him. The great pain was accompanied by an even greater joy.

> **PERSONAL TAKE:** *If we read only verses 7-8, we would emphatically say that Paul would have done anything to get rid of his thorn. But after reading verses 9-10, do you think Paul would remove his thorn or keep his thorn, given the opportunity?*

> **PERSONAL RESPONSE:** *Has God ever given or allowed something painful in your life that you desperately wanted removed, but later wouldn't trade? Perhaps it was even something evil in nature. Record your thoughts below.*

I pray you're encouraged today by this difficult passage. If we weren't given verses 9-10, we might find ourselves despairing over verses 7-8. Imagine if Paul chose to live in the atmosphere of the first two verses, never moving into the hope of Christ's promises and blessings to him. His boasting about his weaknesses would have been lamenting as a martyr. His gladness would have been madness. His delighting in hardships because there he found Christ's strength would have been bitterness over a helpless identity.

Dear sister, if we will choose to seek the Lord's response to our difficulties, whether a persistent thorn or the other hardships mentioned, we will experience the miracle of being glad in sadness, boasting about weakness, and delighting in suffering. Not because we're detaching, compartmentalizing, or blocking out reality. But because we're experiencing the very real presence of Jesus, whose strength is perfected in our weakness.

A dear friend of my family's recently went through one of the most devastating losses a person can endure. He wrote this prayer: "God, you permit what you could have prevented. Thank you. My heart trusts in your unfailing love." This is the miracle I'm talking about. A heart of thanks and trust in the Lord who may give or allow the thorn, but never does so without also giving the grace and power of Jesus in extra measure. For when we're weak, we're strong.

SESSION 7 VIEWER GUIDE

THORN IN THE FLESH

GROUP DISCUSSION:

Why does Paul focus his boasting on his weaknesses? Give an example of what it looks like to boast in your weakness without it being false humility.

Why do we sometimes feel such a need to promote ourselves? How can we defer attention from ourselves to Christ without coming off as a martyr?

Kelly stated, "Our reputation shouldn't be based on a handful of extraordinary experiences but on the long haul of our words and deeds." While we may agree that is true, why do we put more stock in the extraordinary?

Why does God hate pride so much? In what ways do you struggle with pride?

Does the passage on Paul's thorn in the flesh trouble you? If so, why? What truths from the text have comforted you even in the midst of its difficulties?

How has the power of Christ been displayed in your weakness?

What one thing stood out to you from this video?

The music featured in this session is from Kelly's Hymns & Hallelujahs CD. Video sessions and the CD are available for purchase at LIFEWAY.COM/ALLTHINGSNEW

Sundried Tomato *and* Goat Cheese Frittata (serves 6)

INGREDIENTS:

6 eggs

1 cup milk

Salt and pepper

4 ounces goat cheese, broken into large

chunks

¼ cup olive oil, plus more for drizzling

2 cloves garlic, minced

1½ cups sun-dried tomatoes

4 cups arugula, roughly chopped and divided

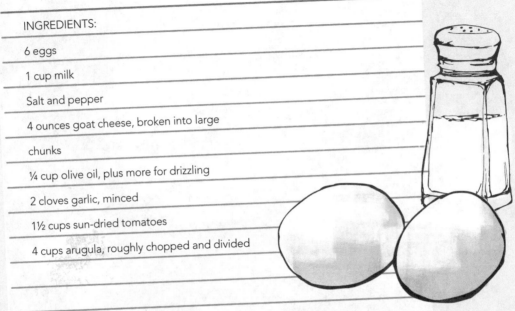

I know some of you meet in the mornings and could use a breakfast recipe, so here's a filling one. A friend made this for me, and I loved it. I kept looking for the crust because it was so filling, but it's all eggs, cheese, and veggies. I also just realized almost every recipe I've chosen shares the common thread of the queen of all ingredients: garlic. You always have my permission to use more than the recipe calls for. Oh, and I haven't given up on finding a dessert that calls for garlic—just give me time.

DIRECTIONS
Preheat oven to 375 degrees.

In a large bowl, whisk together eggs and milk until smooth. Season with salt and pepper to taste. Add goat cheese and stir just enough to coat. Set aside.

Heat ¼ cup olive oil in a large ovenproof skillet over medium heat. Add garlic and sauté about 1 minute. Add sundried tomatoes and 3½ cups arugula, stirring for 1 minute. Pour egg mixture over ingredients in pan and cook about 5 minutes, or until the eggs begin to set.

Transfer the skillet to the preheated oven and bake about 10 to 15 minutes, or until the frittata has set and is slightly golden on top. Remove from the oven and let stand for 5 minutes.

Sprinkle the frittata with the remaining ½ cup arugula leaves and drizzle with olive oil. Slice into wedges and serve.

SESSION 8

SPENDING OURSELVES
FOR OTHERS

As we begin our final week together I pray our theme verse will anchor you for the rest of your days, "Therefore, if anyone is in Christ, he is a new creation. The old has passed away; behold, the new has come" (2 Cor. 5:17, ESV). Who doesn't love the concept of being made new in Christ? Swelling with hope is the image of the old siphoning out to sea as the new sweeps in like rolling waves charging toward the shore. Writing about this reality has further defined my hope as a believer and my expectation for change.

The troubling catch is that as much as the idea lures me in, it also leaves me stymied. What I mean is, I love the reality of being a new person in Christ, but I'm still here with a decent helping of what feels patently old. My family and friends will vouch for me. Sure, I can without a doubt see more Christlikeness defining my life, but still— the old doesn't feel like it's passed away quite like I'd hoped; the new doesn't feel as though it's come quite as decisively as the verse reads.

Let me clarify a bit. Yesterday I was inexcusably irritable with a friend who was helping me with a computer problem. While she hung over my shoulder I could hear her chewing—didn't she realize this was no time for mouth sounds? I've been swatting at critical thoughts toward others, more so than normal, like flies buzzing around in my brain that somehow keep slipping into my thinking. Why can't my thoughts eagerly default to the good work that God is doing in people instead of locking onto what bothers me or where they're falling short? I went to bed last night feeling more not-married than usual,

wondering why my life looks so far outside the bell curve. I could list a few other things, but you know old when you see it. It's so awfully familiar.

Perhaps an old familiar habit is back in your life and it's brought with it its perpetually self-centered cousins, discontentment and negativity. You wonder how Paul can say with surety and aplomb that the old has gone and the new has come, especially when the old seems so present and the new seems to have gotten lost on the way.

So what does a verse like this mean? Remember the context in which Paul was writing was rife with people judging one another by human standards. It was all about how well you performed and what you could achieve and how well you looked while pulling the whole shebang off— you've studied this thoroughly. (The culture was hardly preaching dependence on Jesus.) Paul refuted this human-centered way of thinking by explaining that something revolutionary had happened: The old has gone, the new has come! The new covenant has replaced the old one. We now live by the Spirit instead of the written code. Instead of God dwelling in tents, Jesus dwells in our hearts. And all of creation is under a new order.

So we need not be defined by how well we do based on a behavioral point system, nor do we have to find our worth in our achievements. Rather, a sweeping change happened in the universe when Jesus made us righteous through His death and resurrection. (This is not to mention the formation of a thriving new community called the church, or creation itself having been freed from the old regime of death, one day to be entirely redeemed.)

We're no longer starring in the old play of our selfish desires and lusts. The whole plot changes because we're not content to live for ourselves anymore but for the One who died and was raised for us.

In this context, Paul is painting the grand milieu of redemption with the bold and decisive brushstrokes of "old" and "new." This is big picture stuff. But with the tip of the finest brush in his collection, he dabs upon our individual hearts: "Therefore, if anyone is in Christ, he is a new creation." Things have just gotten exceedingly personal—*if anyone is in Christ*. When we're in Christ, He starts rewriting the script. We're no longer starring in the old play of our selfish desires and lusts. The whole plot changes because we're not content to live for ourselves anymore but for the One who died and was raised for us (2 Cor. 5:15). We now see everyone around us with new eyes because of who each one is in Christ or who each one can be in Him. The big picture redemption of old and new has also touched us individually.

Still you ask, why then am I battling the old stuff when I've been made new? I wonder if the answer isn't tucked away a few verses later in 2 Corinthians 6:1 where Paul urges us not to receive God's grace in vain. Even as a new person in Christ I can choose to live by the old script. I can nurture my pride and slip in a few morsels of gossip at the table and indulge at the troughs of temptation. I can choose the world's company as my closest community and at night lay my head down on the wrong pillow. I can cultivate unforgiveness because it feels safer than the alternative. I'm free to wound those who have hurt me or withhold good from those who need me. In other words, I believe it's possible to be new with old clothes on, though this is positively a miserable way to exist.

Personally, I have struggled with things like a critical spirit, selfishness, and pettiness, to name a few. But when I remember that I am in Christ as a new creation—both of which are states of being, not how well I'm currently performing—I'm propelled to fall into step with the newness Christ has brought about in my heart. I can moment-by-moment choose to comply with the new—to receive God's grace for its intended purpose. It requires some fortitude and starving our selfishness, but there's nothing like growing into the woman Jesus has made you to be. Absolutely nothing like it. And do not for one second believe Satan's lie that you just happen to be the one person on earth for whom Jesus only made a little bit new. Own your new creation-ness.

In day-to-day terms, this means we can put other people's desires ahead of our own, we can course correct our thinking by being in the Word and having our minds renewed, and we will seek the humble heart of Christ instead of our own arrogance and pride. We'll rely on the God-sized power we have to tear down the bars of thinking and behavior that keep us stuck. When we feel unattractive and unchosen we can fall into our Comforter who draws near to us, assuring us we're not alone. When we don't know how to chart our path, He gives wisdom. When we're impatient or critical, we confess and don't have to wonder if we'll be forgiven—restoration is in full supply. When we're attacked we have an arsenal of spiritual weapons at our disposal that are surprisingly powerful.

Yes, everything is different now. Everything is new. All we need to do is receive God's grace so we can live as though it's true.

DAY 1

SPENDING OUR STUFF
AND OURSELVES

2 CORINTHIANS 12:11-18

Welcome to the first day of the last week of *All Things New*! I'm seriously praising God for you. You've persevered, and you're in the process of finishing a good work that will continue to affect lives not only here on earth, but also for eternity. We learned from the opening video that 2 Corinthians was a letter to a church in a city, written out of weakness, with an open heart about how all of life can change because Jesus has made all things new. (We also determined this might be a run-on sentence.) My hope is that you've seen how applicable the gospel is to real life, your life. We've emphasized the message of Christ's strength in our weakness, which I hope you're experiencing as a reality and not just a concept. We've seen Paul keep an open heart, no matter the pain, because nothing was more important than the Corinthians knowing their lives could be made totally new through Jesus, even if he got hurt in the process. And we're not done yet! We're headed into a particularly relational ending to Paul's letter. Let's finish strong!

READ 2 CORINTHIANS 12:11-18.

I love the way verse 11 opens. What reason does Paul give for why he had to make a fool of himself?

Paul's tone reminds me of a story one of my favorite spiritual mothers once told me. Kathy, who's been a missionary in Italy with her family for the past 30 years, was in the piazza of Rome sharing with a belligerent man about the love of Jesus. He goaded her with unanswerable questions, looking for a fight more than a conversation. "Why should I believe Jesus loves me?" was his final retort in a string of objections. Kathy's mother had recently and unexpectedly passed away, and she'd missed her passing because she was serving in Italy. She wasn't in the mood for this guy's belligerence. "Because the Lord took me away from my home in Florida," she protested. "Uprooted my whole family, dropped me in a place I didn't want to come to, stuck me in the middle of all you crazy Italians. That's how you should know that Jesus loves you!" I'm sure he felt the love.

Sometimes, people just drive us to our wit's end. They test us to the uttermost boundaries of our patience. But when we step back from the frustration of giving to people who don't seem to get it, we realize the Lord must really love these people if He's asking us to wear ourselves out like this.

PERSONAL TAKE: *According to today's text, how would you sum up in one sentence the main contention the Corinthians had with Paul?*

There's little more discouraging than when the people you serve tell you there's someone they think ministers a bit better than you. After all Paul had done for the Corinthians, a few of them had abandoned his leadership for the "Super Apostle Bandwagon." This had to be heartbreaking for Paul personally, but even more troubling was how this might unravel the church.

In response to their obsession with the super apostles, Paul mentions three proofs of his apostleship in verse 12. What are they?

1.

2.

3.

As the early church was being born, validating signs, awe-inspiring wonders, and miracles that revealed God's power were proofs of the apostles' spiritual authority.

READ ACTS 14:8-15.

What adverse reaction transpired in Lystra after Paul healed the lame man?

According to verse 15, what was Paul and Barnabas's ultimate goal?

Paul provided supernatural proof of his apostleship in many places, but it didn't always seem to convince unbelieving hearts. As we can see from the dissenters in Corinth, despite what Paul had shown them, some were still following after false apostles.

I believe that the Lord still works wonders and miracles today—and I'm so grateful He does— but I also believe equal if not greater proofs of our faith and discipleship exist. Turn to the following references and note what characteristics show the world we're disciples of Jesus.

John 13:34-35

Galatians 5:22-23

Perhaps you've thought, *if only I could perform a miracle or throw a sign into the sky for someone, I know she'd believe.* Sometimes we wish we could prove our faith by some supernatural happening that would leave no doubt in anyone's mind about the reality of the gospel. Yet, even after Jesus had performed miracles in the midst of the Jews, many of them still didn't believe (John 12:37). While we may wish for an irrefutable miracle to prove the gospel, I believe the way we love people and display the fruit of the Spirit are the most convincing proofs of all. Consider how effective our testimony is when we're ...

1. Content in the Lord in much or in little;

2. Loving each other selflessly;

3. Forgiving when it doesn't make sense;

4. Trusting God's sovereignty in the midst of hardship;

5. Rejoicing in the unseen realities of our hope in Christ;

6. Fill in your own:

While I hope we never stop believing in God's miraculous powers, let's never forget that our love may still be the greatest proof of the gospel.

PERSONAL RESPONSE: *Write the name of one person you know who doesn't know Jesus. What's one way you can live out the "proof" of Jesus' love for that person?*

In verses 13-14, Paul relates how he went out of his way to not be a _____ to the Corinthians.

❏ *burden*
❏ *imposition*

❏ *inconvenience*
❏ *apostle*

Paul didn't want to charge the Corinthian church for his ministry. How did he use a parent/child relationship to illustrate this?

One of the chief complaints of the Corinthians was that Paul wasn't accepting financial support from them. They took this to mean they were inferior to the other churches, when in reality Paul didn't want to put an added burden on them. They should have felt more loved, not less. This issue goes beyond mere missionary or pastoral support. It reveals issues of control and comparison thinking.

Control: The Corinthians wanted Paul to receive financial support from them. As we touched on earlier, how might this be used to control him?

Comparison Thinking: According to verse 13, how did the Corinthians feel they compared to other churches based on the fact Paul had received support from those churches?

Have you ever earnestly tried to show your love to someone only for the person to receive it as something entirely different? One of the more painful experiences of my life was when I made a sacrifice for someone who took it as a slight instead of an act of love.

PERSONAL REFLECTION: *When people mistake my love for something opposite, it can be hurtful, even deeply wounding. How was Paul's response in today's passage drastically different? List the one specific way he responded that challenges and inspires you the most.*

In verse 14 we see that Paul was not after _____. He only wanted _____.

What two-fold blessing did Paul offer them (v. 15)?

PERSONAL REFLECTION: *Which do you find more challenging, spending your actual self on people, or spending your money or resources on them? Explain. (Example: Spending yourself might mean spending an afternoon with someone who needs encouragement or being vulnerable with him or her. Spending what you have may be giving money or something you own to someone in need.)*

Paul was so selfless in serving the Corinthians that I'm not sure they knew what to do with it. It's almost as if they wanted to earn his love and ministry. Sometimes we don't know what to do when someone selflessly serves us, when a person is after our hearts and not our stuff, when he or she gives without looking for something in return. This is where our pride and sense of independence can start squirming. We want to earn people's love and affection, which is really no love at all. Perhaps we're more like the Corinthian church than we think.

PERSONAL RESPONSE: *What barriers keep you from receiving unconditional love and friendship? What specific steps can you take to freely and graciously receive what's being offered without trying to earn the friendship, comparing it to other relationships, or falling into codependency?*

Not only did Paul spend his resources and himself on loving the Corinthians, he sacrificed something else very personal to him. Who did Paul send to Corinth on his behalf (vv. 17-18)?'

We may not fully realize the sacrifice it was for Paul to send some of his dearest friends and ministry partners to visit Corinth. Not only would he miss their day-to-day partnership, but he also had no idea what awaited them nor could he control their fate. I read a biography on the great missionary pioneer, Hudson Taylor, and was amazed at the relationships he sacrificed to bring the glad tidings of the gospel to China. Sharing the gospel can bring great joy, but it can also bring great sacrifice, whether you're letting loved ones go so they can fulfill God's calling, or you're the one who's stepping out. Faith is required for both.

Bottom line, the people we love are most blessed when we release them to the Lord.

Let's take a moment to consider whether we're clinging to any of our relationships too tightly. We don't want to refuse an assignment from God because we can't let go of someone. And neither do we want to hold our loved ones back from God's calling on their lives because of our selfish demands. While releasing those we cherish to follow God's leading will occasionally mean physical separation, much of the time it requires a different kind of sacrifice. It could be a spouse making less money at a different job, a friend who's out an extra night a week for a ministry opportunity, a move that may be challenging (but good) for your children. Bottom line, the people we love are most blessed when we release them to the Lord. And so are we.

PERSONAL RESPONSE: *Ask the Holy Spirit to reveal to you if there's anyone you're holding too tightly. If there is, pray for the grace to release that loved one to the Lord, freeing you both up to do the work God has placed on your lives. I truly believe that our relationships are most full when they're first offered to the Lord.*

DAY 2
THREE FEARS, ONE SOLUTION

2 CORINTHIANS 12:19-21

"I suppose that all Christian workers have found it much easier to lead people out of Egypt, than to get them into the land of Promise."[1] These words were written by Paget Wilkes, an English missionary to Japan who lived from 1871-1934. His point? It's easier to get people to leave their life of sin than to lead them into living the abundant Christian life to its full capacity. Like the Israelites, we're so glad to be free of Egypt's bondage that we settle for life in the desert. It's as if it never occurs to us that the Lord led us out of Egypt (misery of our sin) to get us into the promised land (abundant life in Jesus). Wilkes's quote reminds me of what Paul was dealing with in Corinth. A brand new church had been born and people had been saved, but they were digging their heels into the desert sand of carnality, content to live as immature believers. Today we'll look at what threatened their moving into the full life Jesus came to bring.

READ 2 CORINTHIANS 12:19-21.

As Paul prepares to make his third visit to Corinth, he has four fears. The first is found in verse 20 where he says he's afraid he won't find the Corinthian believers in the good place he hopes. (And—second—if they're in a bad place they won't be all that excited to see him either.)

PERSONAL REFLECTION: *Describe a time when you had anxiety over seeing someone you hadn't seen in awhile. What were your apprehensions? How did you prepare yourself? Did it go as you expected or were you surprised?*

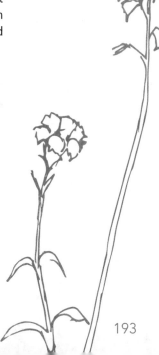

Paul's third fear is finding the church rife with disobedience. Review verse 20 and list the eight sinful behaviors he's afraid he'll find.

1.

2.

3.

4.

5.

6.

7.

8.

PERSONAL TAKE: *Review the list. Which one have you seen cause the most damage in the church and in your personal life? Why?*

Every time I check in at the airport, I'm reminded of all the hazardous materials I'm not supposed to be carrying. The list is extensive, with any one of the items having the ability to cause harm or even bring the plane down, God forbid. I sort of hate being confronted with this list every time I fly because it reminds me of all the things that could go wrong. I miss the days when peanut allergies were the big concern. When it comes to the health of the church, the hazardous materials are not things like lithium batteries, as you well know. They're "quarrels, jealousy, flaring tempers, taking sides, angry words, vicious rumors, swelled heads, and general bedlam" (MSG). May it not be so of us, dear Lord!

It's easy to read a verse like this in the way we glance through the hazardous materials list at the airport—barely paying attention, sure that none of that stuff's in our bag. But let's take a thorough and honest look at the eight destructive behaviors again and make certain none of these are characteristic of us.

PERSONAL REFLECTION: *Review the list, asking the Holy Spirit to show you if any of these behaviors are true of you. I'm doing the same. At whatever point you're convicted, write a confession to the Lord in the margin, remembering that He is faithful and just to forgive and purify you (1 John 1:9). Also, write specific steps you're going to take to make a change.*

I'm amazed at how destructive seemingly harmless sins can be. Things like sharing negative information about someone under the auspice of a prayer request or secretly wishing a person failure because you're jealous of her success, losing your temper when things don't go your way, or fostering arrogance because, after all, the way you do things is so much cooler and relevant than the other person's way. We can justify these behaviors and at times even dress them up to appear spiritual. However, we've just walked a weapon into the holy body that Jesus calls His church. I want us to be people who build up the body of Christ, not tear it down.

Paul mentions his fourth fear in verse 21. What three additional sinful behaviors is he afraid he'll find the Corinthians continuing to engage in?

1.

2.

3.

All three of these are sexual in nature. Turn back to 1 Corinthians 6:18-20. Explain what is particularly destructive about sexual sin, and why it's vital to honor God with our bodies.

Review 2 Corinthians 12:21. I want you to notice a significant concept that's easy to miss. Paul says he's afraid he'll be grieved over those who have not _____ over their sexual sin.

❏ *repented* ❏ *changed*
❏ *stopped* ❏ *paid their dues*

The word *repent* means *to change one's mind for the better,* to literally *turn around* from our sin to an obedient walk with the Lord. Romans 2:4 reminds us that God's kindness is what leads us to repentance. It's His tender hand tapping us on the shoulder—sometimes yanking us by the collar—to save us from destruction and lead us back to His life-giving side. Paul's grief wasn't over the Corinthians' past sexual sins of which they had repented and received forgiveness. He was troubled over the previous pattern of sexual sin some Corinthians were persisting in. There's a difference.

> Or do you despise the riches of His kindness, restraint, and patience, not recognizing that God's kindness is intended to lead you to repentance?
> Romans 2:4, HCSB

PERSONAL RESPONSE: *Choose to answer one of the following.*

OPTION A: *If you struggle with guilty feelings over past sexual sin you've repented of and received forgiveness for, write Colossians 1:22 in the space provided. Know that you've been forgiven and washed clean, and don't allow the enemy to accuse you and defeat you with sins that have been covered by the blood of Jesus.*

OPTION B: *If you're currently struggling with sexual sin, turn to
1 John 1:9 and write the verse in the margin. Sometimes sexual sins can
be more difficult to break free of than other sins because they bind us in
habitual patterns that often require outside help for healing. While we're
forgiven in an instant, becoming free can take time. If you're caught in
sexual sin, the first step is confessing your sin to God and then to a trusted,
loving believer who can help you along the path to freedom. James 5:16
tells us to confess our sins to one another so we can be healed. Repent
today and take the next steps to walk in that repentance.*

While dealing with our sins can be an unpleasant task, it's necessary.
Repentance is required to experience the full life Jesus longs to give us. We
simply can't have His abundant life while hanging onto our sexual addictions
or gossip or hatred or unforgiveness or whatever sin we're clutching. Even
though Paul had three pressing fears concerning the harmful behaviors of
the Corinthians, he started today's passage with an indisputable positive.
Look back at verse 19.

What endearing term does Paul use to refer to the Corinthians?

What motivates Paul to do the things he does for them?

Paul and his friends challenged the people they loved in Corinth because
they considered them dear friends. Many were brothers and sisters in Christ.
They persisted in their ministry because they wanted the Corinthians to be
built up, edified, and strengthened. They didn't minister according to their
own rules or decision-making skills but rather in the sight of God, as people
who lived in the love and boundaries of Christ and His character.

If you're sensing the conviction of the Spirit in regard to any of the sins we've
discussed today, I pray you'll sense God's kindness all over His conviction. I
pray you'll see that turning from the harmful sins that wound others and
yourself is for the sole purpose of turning to the abundant life Jesus has
come to offer. Take absolutely whatever steps are necessary to confess,
repent, and free yourself from any sins you're participating in. Jesus has
already finished the work of making a way for your purity; you need only to
take Him up on it.

DAY 3

THE PROOF
OF CHRIST

2 CORINTHIANS 13:1-4

The final chapter of Paul's letter opens with a word about his upcoming third visit to the Corinthians. To refresh your memory, Paul visited Corinth for the first time in A.D. 50 and stayed how long? (See page 13 for the answer and write it in the margin.) His second visit was what many refer to as the "painful visit," which is mentioned in 2 Corinthians 2:1-2. It was painful because Paul found that the young church had fallen into the strong sway of materialism, immorality, and false beliefs that were popular at the time. As Paul continues to prepare the church for his third visit, he desperately hopes to find them in good standing with himself and, more importantly, with the Lord.

READ 2 CORINTHIANS 13:1-4.

PERSONAL TAKE: *Paul said he would not spare those "who sinned earlier." (This is the same phrase we saw yesterday in 2 Cor. 12:21. It refers to those who were persisting in previous sin without repentance.) Look back at 2 Corinthians 1:23 and compare it with 13:2. Why do you think he spared them earlier but wasn't going to spare them this time?*

Paul comes out swinging here. You may be wondering if his love has run out, if he's finally reached the bottom of his mercy and grace barrel. Remember Paul has been perennially patient. He's spared them, pleaded with them, performed miracles among them, written to them, sent his best friends their way, and visited them personally. He's even taken an Old Testament mandate to extra lengths to make sure he wasn't acting hastily or in error.

Write below the Old Testament law Paul quotes in verse 1, originally given in Deuteronomy 19:15.

In ancient Israelite culture, when someone was accused of committing a sin, the accusation had to be validated by two or more witnesses. This helped confirm the facts and safeguard anyone from being falsely accused or wrongly punished. I believe Paul is using this passage metaphorically, meaning that his previous two visits, two warnings, and upcoming visit serve as the 2-3 witnesses needed to establish a conviction. In other words, Paul had been as thorough, patient, and measured as possible, but now it was time to deal with the sin that was harming the church.

Sometimes I'm guilty of judging people based only on rumors. Other times I'm guilty of not confronting those who are harming themselves with their decisions.

> **PERSONAL REFLECTION:** *How does Paul's balance of patiently investigating the problems in Corinth and his willingness to decisively deal with those problems challenge you? In other words, how can you be slower to judge when you don't know all the facts, yet quicker to lovingly confront when you do?*

When I look at today's verses I see one word at the heart of the chaos and conflict in Corinth. (Fill in the blank below.)

I already gave you a warning when I was with you the second time. I now repeat it while absent: On my return I will not spare those who _____ earlier or any of the others (2 Cor. 13:2).

When my niece Maryn was six years old, she had this great conversation with my sister Katie on the way home from Sunday school. "Mom," she asked from the backseat of the car, "what is sin?"

"Well, it's that thing we've talked about when you don't share with your brother, or you talk back to Mommy and Daddy," Katie said while maneuvering traffic. "Sometimes when you know you've done something wrong you have that bad feeling we've talked about."

"Oh yeah, I remember now," Maryn affirmed. Like, she had this sin thing down. A couple hours went by and Katie had all but forgotten the conversation when Maryn approached her with all her Italian hand gestures (my sister married a New Jersey Italian), "Mom, Judah ran his big wheel into my tricycle today just to be mean." Pausing a second, she emphatically continued, "I mean, talk about SIN!"

easter egg hunt

Come join the fun!

The church wide Easter Egg Hunt

will be held on April 15th from 11:00 a.m. to 12:30 p.m.

Open to pre-school through 5th grade age children.

Thank you to those who have donated candy!!

Youth Pretzel Sales

The youth will be selling pretzels, now until Easter
following Sunday Service.

Easter Sunrise Service

APRIL 16, 2017
6:40 A.M.

MEMORIAL PARK
E. STATE ST.
ALLIANCE, OHIO

BREAKFAST TO FOLLOW
8:00 A.M.

FIRST CHURCH OF GOD
505 N. LINCOLN AVE.
ALLIANCE, OHIO

I second Maryn's sentiments—talk about some sin in Corinth! Some of the Corinthians had been reveling in it and drawing others into their swirl. Sin—it's the ruthless thing we deal with. It's the thing that ruins relationships, dissolves trust, fuels jealousy, stirs selfishness, harbors unforgiveness, and fractures goodness. Praise God, He has made a way for us to escape its captivity.

In verses 3-4, Paul mentions the crucifixion and resurrection of Jesus, His weakness and His power. Paul brings this up because a few of the ungodly leaders in Corinth had apparently questioned whether Jesus was really speaking through Paul. Paul's response was that Jesus was surely powerful among them and would not be weak in dealing with them. Recently I've been mindful of the Lord's gracious dealings with me in times of wandering and disobedience. I wasn't particularly grateful for the discipline at the time, but looking back I'm so thankful He was powerful in rescuing me from my sin.

> **PERSONAL REFLECTION:** *How has Jesus specifically shown His power in dealing with sin or temptation in your life? After you write a brief description, spend some time thanking Him for His active power working in your life.*

Look back at verse 3. What were the Corinthians demanding from Paul?

I've been thinking a lot lately about what the proof of Jesus' activity in our lives looks like. The other day I ran into someone at the store I hadn't seen in a while. He's had a lot of success in Christian media and just landed another huge deal. One of the things he said was, "I'm just really enjoying God's favor right now." Please hear me say I'm not judging God's favor on a person's life—this large deal could very well be part of God's blessing on my acquaintance. But it gave me pause. Is the proof of Jesus' hand on our lives found only in big money, big deals, flashes of fame, and our biggest dreams coming true? Or is the proof of His power also found in us when we are given grace to love the unlovely, adopt a child when we're scared to death, forgive when it flies in the face of our gut reaction, and hear His Holy Spirit whisper tender words of affirmation to our broken hearts?

The church at Corinth was still looking for Paul to come with showy signs and demonstrative expressions of power, maybe even wealth. I think we sometimes look for the same types of things in our lives to decide if Jesus is

really present in us—or in someone else. Again, we see Paul bring a mystery back around that I hope we'll never forget: Christ reigned by God's power and He was crucified in weakness. In the same way, Paul had several areas of weakness in his life, yet God's power was extraordinarily strong in Him.

PERSONAL REFLECTION: *Have you ever considered that your weaknesses could actually be proof of Christ's hand on your life, because in those areas He wants to show Himself strong? Explain.*

I truly don't believe Paul is advocating for a brand of Christianity where everyone is incompetent, unskilled, and dead broke because we're trying to avoid anything that looks like strength or success. That is not what it means to be weak in Christ. In the areas where we are truly weak, we can rely on the power of God to operate in our weakness. And where we are strong in this world, we offer that strength to God as if it were weakness because even our greatest strength is not as strong as the weakness of God (1 Cor. 1:25). Our expertise, accomplishments, and wealth, while good things, cannot be the sole proof of His favor on our lives. What Paul expressed in Philippians 3 is that none of our strengths compare to knowing Christ.

Dear follower of Christ, make sure you're not judging the proof of God's hand on your life merely by outward, materialistic blessings. As we've seen throughout 2 Corinthians, oftentimes His greatest display of power in our lives is in our places of loneliness, battles with infirmities, and painful losses. Whether you're feeling weak or strong, hide yourself as weak in Christ, as a child is weak when resting in her father's arms. This is where we'll find the true strength to love God and serve others.

DAY 4
PASSING
THE TEST
2 CORINTHIANS 13:5-10

READ 2 CORINTHIANS 13:5-10.

Focus for a moment on verse 5. What are your thoughts and emotions as you ponder this verse?

Verses like 13:5 used to throw me into a tailspin of fear and uncertainty. *Have I passed the test? Am I really a true Christian? What if I've been disqualified and I don't know it? How can I know if Jesus is really in me?* If these troubling thoughts haven't already crossed your mind, I'm glad I've now made you aware. I wish I'd known at the time that Paul meant this to be an affirming question, carrying the idea of "proving in the expectation of approving."[2] In other words, Paul wanted the Corinthians to take a hard look at themselves with the expectation they would discover that Jesus Christ was truly in their lives and working in their midst. As a result, they would also see Paul as an authentic minister of Christ and would orient their lives around the truth He'd been teaching them.

The reason for examining and testing is to discover the true nature or character of something, to determine its genuineness.[3] So when Paul talks about testing and examining yourself he speaks in terms of a person being qualified as a true believer. The hopeful expectation is that a person is tested and found to have a genuine faith.

It would be as if your high school math teacher, right before passing out final exams said, "Class, don't you realize how smart and accomplished you are? You've applied yourself all year! I want you to take this test because it's going to prove to you everything you've learned. I have no doubt you'll succeed." You would receive this as encouragement and inspiration, making you eager to take the test. The positive test result would more substantially prove what was already there.

PERSONAL REFLECTION: *Take your time in answering these questions: What are some of the greatest desires of your heart? What spiritual passions most drive you? How is your heart moved to sacrificially love others? What motivates your prayers? What obedient actions are you taking?*

Your answers to the previous questions should help you recognize Jesus' activity in your life. One way I see Christ's presence in my life is how He's changed my passions and desires. So much sanctification still needs to take place, but I find myself more earnest than before for ministry over materialism, people over pleasures, Christ over comfort. I know this can only be a result of Jesus in me.

While Paul's desire was for the Corinthians to examine themselves to affirm Jesus Christ was truly in their midst, he couldn't possibly know the spiritual state of every person who'd hear his letter. Thus the phrase, "unless you fail the test." Meaning, there might be a few who would examine themselves and realize they'd never come into relationship with Jesus, they'd never looked to Him to cleanse them of their sins, and had no desire to live according to Paul's apostolic teaching. If you're concerned about whether or not you're in the faith, the good news of the gospel is that in order to pass the test, you simply have to trust in the Savior who passed it for you. We'll get to this at the close of today's study.

Read verses 6-7 again. What does Paul hope the Corinthians will finally discover about him and his fellow ministers?

I find verse 7 convicting. Paul desperately hoped the Corinthians would stop sinning so they could do what was right, but not for the ultimate purpose of him looking good. If they didn't shape up he would have the opportunity to really show off his spiritual authority. But he was far more concerned about their spiritual health than his own reputation. He would rather they repent on their own so he could visit them as a gentler Paul instead of getting to wield his authority chops.

PERSONAL REFLECTION: *Is there anyone in your life you hope will get his or her act together more for your sake than for theirs? Ask the Lord to purify your motives in this relationship.*

As we disciple and come alongside others, it's important for us to evaluate our heart's motives. I've often wanted the people around me to align their Christian beliefs closer to mine or clean up their behavior more for my benefit and reputation than out of genuine concern for their relationship with Christ. Sometimes I want to help people because I'll come off looking extra wise and spiritual. At other times my biggest concern is having people on my theological side. For Paul, even if he looked like a failure he didn't care. He just wanted the people he loved so dearly to stop their destructive behavior so they could live righteously for Jesus. My hope is that I'm becoming more like this, with my priority to grow up others in the Lord, regardless of my reputation.

> *Review verse 8 and fill in the blank.*
> *Whether Paul finds the Corinthians in blatant sin or in humble repentance, when he arrives he'll act according to the _____.*

PERSONAL TAKE: *Review verses 9-10. What do you think Paul meant when he said he's happy when he's weak and the Corinthians are strong?*

Growing up with my parents in ministry meant seeing some difficult confrontations over the years. Neither one of my parents took joy in slinging their ministerial authority around or coming off as large and in charge. I know my dad would rather humbly teach and shepherd his people as they served the Lord versus having to authoritatively confront those who were causing division. In similar fashion, Paul's desire for the Corinthians to be restored trumped his concern for how they viewed him. He would much prefer the people perceive him as weak, rather than having to show off his authoritative strength. He wanted to come with gentle authority to build them up, not tear them down.

PERSONAL RESPONSE: *Answer one of the following.*

OPTION A: *Do you naturally like to confront, be in charge, make people abide by the rules? How can you temper these actions with a grace that's more concerned for people's wellbeing than for you being right and in charge?*

OPTION B: *Do you tend to avoid confrontation at all costs? Do you let problems fester longer than you should? What steps will you take to be more bold and deal with things head-on instead of avoiding?*

However you're led to use your authority, remember it's given by God and for building others up.

I hope the Lord is piercing your heart for people and their spiritual growth. My desire is that He's convicting you to show grace before punishment, to give the benefit of the doubt before judgment, and to see the good of others as superior to your personal gain. I also hope that if you hesitate to stand up for what's right or confront someone who's in sin, you'll find courage to step up if need be. However you're led to use your authority, remember it's given by God and for building others up. Keep in mind that this will look different in different situations.

I want to close today's study by going back to verse 5. There Paul challenged the Corinthians to examine themselves to make sure they were true believers. He made this request with the optimistic expectation that they'd realize anew Jesus Christ was in them.

While I believe many of the original hearers of the letter were found confident in their faith, I also believe some who heard this question needed to come to Jesus Christ and receive Him as Savior. Perhaps the same is true today. If you don't know Christ, nothing would make me happier than to know you placed your faith in Jesus today and received Him as your Savior. And if you're already a believer, what joyful affirmation to once again recognize Jesus in your midst.

PERSONAL RESPONSE: *So let's make the challenge personal: Examine yourself to see if you are in the faith. The challenge is not meant to bring fear or raise doubt. Rather it's to encourage and assure. Is your faith for salvation placed solely on Christ and His finished work on the cross? If so, you are "in the faith." If not, receive His forgiveness and trust Him alone for your salvation today.*

Paul says in Acts 13:38-39,

> **"Therefore, let it be known to you, brothers, that through [Jesus] forgiveness of sins is being proclaimed to you, and everyone who believes in Him is justified from everything that you could not be justified from through the law of Moses." (HCSB)**

Yesterday I went to my mailbox and pulled out a letter from a 12-year-old boy named Daniel who goes to my parent's church. Daniel was born with a brain tumor and has recently gone blind as a result. The letter was written in Braille. He wrote to thank me for singing "Happy Birthday" to him the week before. Here are his precious and poignant words:

"Kelly, thank you for singing to me. Do you know Jesus? Love, Daniel."

Paul asked the Corinthians. Daniel asked me. And today I have asked you: Do you know Jesus?

DAY 5
GRACE, LOVE, & FELLOWSHIP

2 CORINTHIANS 13:11-14

A lot of life has happened since I first gave myself to studying and teaching 2 Corinthians. You know how that goes. We have our jobs, the daily mundane activities, perhaps a trying hardship, along with some really joyous occasions and celebratory milestones. It's in the midst of all this life that what I really believe about the truths of 2 Corinthians has been tested. Truths such as God's comfort in pain, His power through the weak vessel of my being, Christ's sufficient grace in enduring trials. Will I love people, even the difficult ones, with my heart stretched a little wider? Do I consider giving a burden or a tremendous privilege? Am I serving others with the power and life of new covenant ministry?

As we come to the end of a journey, I want to finish by returning to where we started. 2 Corinthians was written to real people in a real city because the gospel is meant to thrive in real life. My prayer is that what we've learned along the way will not be mere academic knowledge but will be put into practice. I don't think Paul would have written 2 Corinthians for anything less than for the church to live it. For us to live it.

PERSONAL REFLECTION: *What single thing from 2 Corinthians has challenged you the most?*

As we finish our final day of homework together, let's read Paul's closing words to the Corinthian church.

READ 2 CORINTHIANS 13:11-13.

Paul leaves the Corinthians with five imperatives (commands) in verse 11. List them below. (Because translations vary, I've included the HCSB translation in the margin for you to work from.)

1. Rejoice (farewell or goodbye)

2.

3.

4.

5.

> Finally, brothers, rejoice. Become mature, be encouraged, be of the same mind, be at peace, and the God of love and peace will be with you.
> 2 Corinthians 13:11, HCSB

PERSONAL TAKE: *Knowing the difficulties in the Corinthian church, which of the five commands do you think would be the most challenging for them and why?*

After Paul's first directive to rejoice, he called the Corinthians to become mature or to reach for restoration. The community of believers in Corinth had settled for something short of the fullness of restoration to God. This simple phrase is more meaningful than we may give it credit for. Paul was pushing them to keep pressing toward spiritual maturity and be equipped and fitted for ministry. Just this morning I confessed to the Lord how easily satisfied I can be with status-quo Christianity, both individually and within my community of believers. I may try to get by with a quick quiet time with the Lord, church attendance, time with friends, dinners with community throughout the week, and some entertainment here or there. I can settle for being out of the pit of sin but not fully in a place of thriving spiritual maturity. But we see in verse 11 we're to press, aim, reach to become spiritually grown up—especially within our believing communities. I really believe one of the messages Paul wants to get across is, "Don't settle!"

PERSONAL RESPONSE: *After completing this study, how can you help the church community you're a part of keep from settling spiritually?*

How does Paul's third command relate to 2 Corinthians 1:3-7? Describe different ways we can put this into practice.

I find the fourth directive to be a little tricky. I would wholeheartedly love to be of one mind with everyone. Of course, as long as they all agreed with me. But this is rarely the case, as you well know.

Read Romans 15:5. How do the concepts of comfort/encouragement and agreement/unity go together?

PERSONAL TAKE: *What are some possible characteristics of a body of believers that is of one mind or in agreement with one another?*

Being of one mind doesn't necessarily mean we all agree on every point or doctrine of the Christian faith. Now, we should always agree on the essentials, holding to the fundamentals of the faith, such as the death and resurrection of Jesus, His Godhead, and salvation being found in Him and Him alone. While there may be room for disagreement over secondary and tertiary issues, our fellowship together must always be characterized by Christian virtues, such as humility, kindness, gentleness, compassion, patience, and others. We may have differing opinions on some important issues, but the non-negotiable abiding fruit of the Spirit we must always strive to have in common. Above all, we should put on love.

PERSONAL REFLECTION: *In your relationships, how does the fifth command flow out of the previous one?*

What is the result of living out these five instructions, according to the end of verse 11?

Paul's second-to-last thoughts revolve around the warmth of community unique to the family of Christ: "Greet one another with a holy kiss. All the saints greet you" (HCSB). While greeting one another with kisses was common to both Jews and Greeks at the time, the holy kiss seemed to originate with Paul. It signaled the affection found in a family that opened its arms wide to any person from any race, culture, or background who named Christ as Savior. No family on earth is as diverse or welcoming as the family of Christ.

No family on earth is as diverse or welcoming as the family of Christ.

Do you see the significance of a holy kiss amidst a fragmented and broken community? It's hard to kiss someone you're mad at or in strong disagreement with. And a holy kiss means you can't fake it while having impure or hostile motives.

Paul extended confidence and grace letting the Corinthians know that all the saints (most likely the Macedonians) send their greetings. Even though the Corinthian church had struggled, Paul counted them among the saints, worthy to receive the Macedonian church's warm affection. This gracious closing shows Paul still saw the Corinthians as true brothers and sisters in the Lord despite the pain and difficult relationships. He still considered them family.

> *I can't think of a better ending to 2 Corinthians—to this beautiful journey we've taken together—than the way Paul closes this letter. Draw a line between each member of the Trinity and the corresponding blessing Paul mentions.*

Jesus   *Grace*

God   *Fellowship*

Holy Spirit   *Love*

PERSONAL TAKE: *Why do you think Paul starts with the grace of Jesus?*

Nowhere else does Paul leave such a strong picture of the Trinity. Despite the problems in Corinth, no division of pain or hardship could overcome the grace, love, and fellowship of Jesus Christ, God the Father, and the Holy Spirit. Paul doesn't end the letter by focusing on himself because he knows that he is not the answer the church needs. His only hope for the church at Corinth is the same hope to which we cling today: the grace of Jesus, who lifted the burden of sin from our shoulders and draped us in His robes of righteousness. He pointed to the love of God the Father that was demonstrated when He sent His one and only Son to earth to be the atonement for our sin and the fellowship of the Holy Spirit who communes with us, teaches us all things, comforts us, and reminds us that we're never alone.

I want to echo Paul's benediction as we link arms across the finish line of this study. May the grace of Jesus meet you at every step, may you be bundled in the love of God, and may the Holy Spirit commune with you in places no human can reach. And if I may borrow from an earlier portion of Paul's letter, whenever you are weak may you find Christ in you as gloriously strong. For since His coming, the old order of powerlessness in sin and brokenness is passed away; behold, all things have been made new.

SESSION 8 VIEWER GUIDE

SPENDING OURSELVES FOR OTHERS

GROUP DISCUSSION:

Have you ever been guilty of wanting what people can give you, rather than just wanting them? Explain.

How would our relationships change if we were willing to not just spend for people but be spent for them? What's the difference?

In what ways are you currently strengthening and encouraging the people around you? Why is it so easy to lose sight of our need to do this? What's the main thing that hinders you?

How willing are you to confront difficult people and difficult situations? What can we learn from both Paul's restraint and readiness when it comes to properly confronting?

Verse 5 tells us to examine ourselves to see if we are in the faith. Does this verse scare you? Encourage you? Kelly explained the gospel message and gave you an opportunity to respond. If you trusted Christ as your Savior, consider sharing that news with your group.

What one thing stood out to you from this video?

The music featured in this session is from Kelly's Hymns & Hallelujahs *CD. Video sessions and the CD are available for purchase at* **LIFEWAY.COM/ALLTHINGSNEW**

Sometimes it behooves you to grab your mom's church cookbook from the 80s, the one that's splattered with three decades of sauce and smudged with grease, where church moms have their names printed next to their prized recipes. This is pure gold. Here's a blast from the past that doesn't need any newfangled ingredients added.

Old School Peanut Butter Brownies (serves 12)

BROWNIE INGREDIENTS	ICING INGREDIENTS:
2 cups flour	1 stick of butter
2 teaspoons baking powder	6 tablespoons milk
2/3 cups butter	4 tablespoons cocoa
1 cup peanut butter (I use crunchy)	1 (16-ounce) box powdered sugar
1 cup sugar	
1 cup brown sugar	
4 eggs	
1 teaspoon vanilla	

BROWNIE DIRECTIONS

Preheat oven to 350 degrees. Mix flour and baking soda together and set aside. Beat butter, peanut butter, and sugars together. Add eggs one at a time. Add vanilla. Once mixed, fold dry ingredients into wet.

Spread the mixture into a greased 13x9x2-inch pan. Bake for 25 to 30 minutes. Brownies are done when they just begin to pull away from the sides of the pan and are set in the center. Cool while you make the chocolate icing.

ICING DIRECTIONS

Melt butter in saucepan with milk and cocoa. Stir. When bubbly, take off heat and add a box of powdered sugar. Whisk until smooth. Spread on cooled brownies and serve.

Leader Guide
INTRODUCTION

All Things New: A Study on 2 Corinthians is a video and discussion based Bible study as part of The Living Room Series. The weekly personal study along with the teaching videos will promote honest conversation as you study Scripture together. Since conversation is essential to the experience, I've written a few starter questions in both the Viewer Guides and Leader Guide to help get the discussion rolling.

The added recipes encourage groups to eat together because so many great friendships and conversations naturally begin around a dinner table. That said, this study may be used in a variety of large or small group settings including churches, homes, offices, coffee shops, or other desirable locations.

TIPS ON LEADING THIS BIBLE STUDY

PRAY: As you prepare to lead *All Things New*, remember that prayer is essential. Set aside time each week to pray for the women in your group. Listen to their needs and the struggles they're facing so you can bring them before the Lord. Though organizing and planning are important, protect your time of prayer before each gathering. Encourage your women to include prayer as part of their own daily spiritual discipline, as well.

GUIDE: Accept women where they are, but also set expectations that motivate commitment. Be consistent and trustworthy. Encourage women to follow through on the study, attend the group sessions, and engage with the homework. Listen carefully, responsibly guide discussion, and keep confidences shared within the group. Be honest and vulnerable by sharing what God is teaching you throughout the study. Most women will follow your lead and be more

willing to share and participate when they see your transparency. Reach out to women of different ages, backgrounds, and stages of life. This is sure to make your conversation and experience richer.

CONNECT: Stay engaged with the women in your group. Use social media, emails, or a quick note in the mail to connect with them and share prayer needs throughout the week. Let them know when you are praying specifically for them. Root everything in Scripture and encourage them in their relationship with Jesus.

CELEBRATE: At the end of the study, celebrate what God has done by having your group share what they've learned and how they've grown. Pray together about what further steps God may be asking you to take as a result of this study.

TIPS ON ORGANIZING THIS BIBLE STUDY

TALK TO YOUR PASTOR OR MINISTER OF EDUCATION: If you're leading this as part of a local church, ask for their input, prayers, and support.

SECURE YOUR LOCATION: Think about the number of women you can accommodate in the designated location. Reserve any tables, chairs, or media equipment for the videos, music, and additional audio needs.

PROVIDE CHILDCARE: If you are targeting moms of young children and/or single moms, this is essential.

PROVIDE RESOURCES: Order leader kits and the needed number of Bible study books. You might get a few extra for last minute sign-ups.

PLAN AND PREPARE: Become familiar with the Bible study resource and leader helps available. Preview the video session and prepare the outline you will follow to lead the group meeting based on the leader helps available. Go to *lifeway.com/AllThingsNew* to find free extra leader and promotional resources for your study.

EVALUATE

At the end of each group session, ask: What went well? What could be improved? Did you see women's lives transformed? Did your group grow closer to Christ and to one another?

NEXT STEPS

Even after the study concludes, follow up and challenge women to stay involved through another Bible study, church opportunity, or anything that will continue their spiritual growth and friendships. Provide several options of ministry opportunities the members can participate in individually or as a group to apply what they have learned through this study.

SESSION 1

1. Welcome women to the study and distribute Bible study books.

2. Watch the Session 1 video, encouraging the women to take notes as Kelly teaches.

3. Following the video, lead women through the Group Discussion section of the Session 1 Viewer Guide (p. 9).

4. Close the session with prayer.

SESSION 2

1. Welcome the women to Session 2 of *All Things New*. Use the following questions to review their previous week's personal study.

   How would you compare the Corinthian culture to our culture today?

   What specifically about our culture makes it difficult to live a holy life? To share your faith?

   How have you experienced the comfort of Christ? And how have you had opportunity to pass along that comfort to someone in need? How do you respond to someone when you've been criticized or misunderstood? What can

we learn from the way Paul responded in the same situation?

   Would you say that you are a sincere, honest person? Would others say that? Explain. Why is this important in your witness for Christ?

   When you face a difficult situation in a relationship, are you more likely to confront or avoid? What do we learn from Paul about confronting but doing so with grace and forgiveness?

2. Watch the Session 2 video, encouraging the women to take notes as Kelly teaches.

3. Following the video, lead women through the Group Discussion section of the Session 2 Viewer Guide (p. 36).

4. Close: Provide an opportunity for any women who are currently suffering or going through difficulty to share their situation. Spend time as a group praying specifically for each woman who shares.

SESSION 3

1. Welcome your group to Session 3 of *All Things New*. Use the following questions to review their previous week's personal study.

   What does it mean to be the aroma of Christ? Is that the fragrance you are spreading? Explain.

   Paul said we are ministers of a new covenant. What did he mean?

   Where does our competency to minister come from? What could be the consequences of ministering in our own power?

   Why has God put the treasure of His message in jars of clay?

   How did Paul encourage the Corinthians not to lose heart during their suffering (2 Cor. 4:16-18)?

What prevents you from viewing your suffering through this lens?

2. Watch the Session 3 video, encouraging the women to take notes as Kelly teaches.

3. Following the video, lead women through the Group Discussion section of the Session 3 Viewer Guide (p. 66).

4. Close: Direct participants to choose a partner. Provide a few minutes for each pair to share their joys and fears about being ministers of the new covenant. Encourage them to pray for one another that they would be bold in their ministry.

SESSION 4

1. Welcome your group to Session 4 of *All Things New*. Use the following questions to review their previous week's personal study.
   What does the word home *mean to you?*

   When you think of all that the word home *means to you, how much does the presence of Jesus factor into that?*

   Knowing you will stand before the judgment seat of Christ, are you challenged? Encouraged? Frightened? Explain.

   What does it mean that the love of Christ compels us? Is it compelling you? Explain.

   Do you really believe that Jesus can make all things new? What is the evidence of that in your life?
   Have you ever written someone off as being too sinful, too stubborn, or too hardhearted to be saved? Explain.

   What does it mean to be an ambassador for Christ? How would you rate your job performance in that area?

How does sharing the gospel keep your life as a believer fresh and exciting?

As a child of God, why is having a binding, intimate relationship with an unbeliever incompatible?

How can we see the command to not be unequally yoked as a positive?

2. Watch the Session 4 video, encouraging the women to take notes as Kelly teaches.

3. Following the video, lead women through the Group Discussion section of the Session 4 Viewer Guide (p. 96).

4. Close: Provide time for women to prayerfully evaluate their current close relationships. Encourage them to consider who in their circle needs to hear the gospel, who has needs that they could meet, and what relationships might need to be adjusted or even severed because of spiritual incompatibility. Pray over the group that they would have courage to be obedient to the Spirit's prompting.

SESSION 5

1. Welcome your group to Session 5 of *All Things New*. Use the following questions to review their previous week's personal study.
   What is the difference between worldly sorrow and godly sorrow?

   When was a time godly sorrow led you to repent, seek God's forgiveness, and change your ways?

   Kelly said "Christian relationships are not easy, but they're worth it." How is this true in your life?

   In a nutshell, what is your view of giving?

   How is it possible for seemingly opposites like joy and extreme poverty to overflow into generosity?

How is Jesus our example for generous giving?

What causes a disconnect between your willingness to give and actually following through?

What do you love most about ministering together with people who share your passion for the poor, lost, or hurting?

2. Watch the Session 5 video, encouraging the women to take notes as Kelly teaches.

3. Following the video, lead women through the Group Discussion section of the Session 5 Viewer Guide (p. 124).

4. Close: Provide an opportunity for your group to give. Briefly discuss what they would want to give toward. It could be a specific ministry in your church, a mission effort, a need in your community or in your group. Take up your offering this week and/or next week.

SESSION 6

1. Welcome your group to Session 6 of *All Things New*. Use the following questions to review their previous week's personal study.

Share a time when you were excited to give toward something, but didn't follow through. What happened? What got in the way? How can you be more accountable?

Which of the three questions on page 135 challenges you the most? Explain. (Read 2 Corinthians 9:8 aloud.) Do you really believe this? Explain.

Review the "11 Truths about Generosity" on page 123. Which of these stands out to you the most and why?

Is there a current situation in your life where you're trying to fight a spiritual battle with worldly weapons? How has this been ineffective?

Why are we so prone to judge our pastors and spiritual leaders by worldly standards? How can we specifically encourage them instead?

What causes us to be jealous over someone else's calling or ministry assignment? How do we keep from going down this road?

2. Watch the Session 6 video, encouraging the women to take notes as Kelly teaches.

3. Following the video, lead women through the Group Discussion section of the Session 6 Viewer Guide (p. 154).

4. Close: Direct women to divide into small groups and share how God has torn down strongholds in their lives. Suggest they also share about current battles they are facing, and pray they have the freedom to do so. Encourage small groups participants to pray for one another.

SESSION 7

1. Welcome your group to Session 7 of *All Things New*. Use the following questions to review their previous week's personal study.

How does Paul use the word jealous in a positive way?

In what ways do you find your biblical worldview being opposed?

Have you ever felt pressured to change your ministry approach or the way you expressed love based on what a specific person wanted? What were the results?

Have you ever encountered non-believers promoting and flaunting their false beliefs? How did you respond? How can you graciously yet boldly boast about Jesus and what He's done in your life?

Why would Paul choose to boast about his weaknesses instead of his strengths?

What are your thoughts and questions, about Paul's thorn in the flesh?

Has God ever given or allowed something painful in your life that you desperately wanted removed, but now wouldn't trade? Explain.

2. Watch the Session 7 video, encouraging the women to take notes as Kelly teaches.

3. Following the video, lead women through the Group Discussion section of the Session 7 Viewer Guide (p. 182).

4. Close: Allow participants to share experiences of when God proved Himself strong in their weaknesses and His grace was sufficient. Offer prayers of thanks and praise for God's faithful work in your lives.

SESSION 8

1. Welcome your group to Session 8 of *All Things New.* Use the following questions to review their previous week's personal study.

   Which do you find more challenging, spending your actual self on people or spending your money or resources on them?

   Are you holding on too tight to a relationship? If so, how is it affecting your walk with Christ and ministry for Him?

   What does it mean to repent? Why is repentance so vital to our Christian lives?

   How has Jesus shown His power in dealing with sin or temptation in your life?

   Review 2 Corinthians 13:5. What are your thoughts and emotions concerning this verse?

   How do you recognize Jesus' activity in your life?

What does it mean to settle spiritually? How can you help your small group and church from settling spiritually?

2. Watch the Session 8 video, encouraging the women to take notes as Kelly teaches.

3. Following the video, lead women through the Group Discussion section of the Session Viewer Guide (p. 210).

4. Close: Provide a time for women to receive Christ. Review the call to salvation Kelly issued on the video. Following this time, spend a moment allowing women to share what they had gained from this study. Pray together thanking God for His truth and the power to live it out.

ENDNOTES

SESSION 2:

1. George H. Guthrie, *Baker Exegetical Commentary On The New Testament,* 2 Corinthians (Grand Rapids, MI: Baker Publishing Group, 2015), 19-23.
2. Ralph P. Martin, *Word Biblical Commentary,* Vol. 40, 2 Corinthians (Nashville, TN: Thomas Nelson, 1986), xxix.
3. Ibid.
4. "Hagiazō," *The New Strong's Exhaustive Concordance of the Bible, BlueLetterBible.com* (online) [cited 12 August 2016]. Available from the Internet: *BlueLetterBible.com.*
5. Guthrie, 15.
6. "Oiktirmos," *Vines Expository Dictionary of New Testament Words, BlueLetterBible.com* (online) [cited 12 August 2016]. Available from the Internet: *BlueLetterBible.com.*
7. Charles H. Spurgeon, *Mornings and Evenings with Spurgeon,* eds. Larry and Marion Pearce (Green Forest, AR: New Leaf Publishing Group, 2010), February 12, Morning.
8. Guthrie, 102.
9. David E. Garland, *The New American Commentary,* Vol. 29, 2 Corinthians (Nashville, TN: B&H Publishing Group, 1999), 103.
10. Ibid.
11. Guthrie, 111.

SESSION 3:

1. Wyn Cooper, Sheryl Crow, David Baerwald, Bill Bottrell and Kevin Gilbert. "All I Wanna Do." *Tuesday Night Music Club.* UMG Recordings, Inc., 1993, compact disc.
2. Guthrie, 41.
3. Spiros Zodhiates, *The Complete Word Study Dictionary: New Testament* (Chattanooga, TN: AMG Publishers, 2000), 479.
4. Guthrie, 205.
5. W.E. Vine, *Vine's Expository Dictionary of New Testament Words* (Nashville: Thomas Nelson, 1996), electronic version. (Italics mine)
6. Harper Lee, *To Kill a Mockingbird* (New York, NY: Grand Central Publishing, 1960), 60.
7. Guthrie, 269, 272.

SESSION 4:

1. C. S. Lewis, *The Weight of Glory* (online) 8 June 1942 [cited 24 August 2016]. Available on the Internet: *verber.com/mark/xian/weight-of-glory. pdf.*
2. "synechō," *BlueLetterBible.com* (online) [cited 12 August 2016]. Available from the Internet: *BlueLetterBible.com.*
3. Guthrie, 293.
4. "Reconcile/Reconciled," *BlueLetterBible.com.*
5. Guthrie, 309.
6. Ibid., 328.
7. Ibid., 329.
8. "Yoke," *Merriam-Webster's Collegiate Dictionary.* 11th ed. Springfield, MA: Merriam-Webster, 2003. Also available at *http://www.merriam-webster.com/.*

SESSION 5:

1. Martin, 220.
2. Guthrie, 363.
3. Guthrie, 381.

SESSION 6

1. Guthrie, 436.
2. C. H. Spurgeon, *The Sword and the Trowel* (London: Passmore & Alabaster, 1873), 126.
3. Guthrie, 472.
4. Ibid., 475.
5. Ibid.
6. Martin, 306.
7. "Practical," *Merrian-Webster's.*
8. "Praotes," Vine.
9. "Epieikeia," Vine.
10. Guthrie, 467.
11. "Praotēs," Vine.

SESSION 7

1. Martin H. Manser, "Jealousy," *Dictionary of Bible Themes* (online) [cited 15 September 2016]. Available from the Internet: *https://www. biblegateway.com/resources/dictionary-of-bible- themes/8773-jealousy*
2. Timothy Savage, *Power Through Weakness* (Cambridge: Cambridge University Press, 1996), 87.
3. Guthrie, 551.
4. Ibid., 582.
5. Ibid., 590.
6. Martin, 412.

SESSION 8

1. Paget Wilkes, *Sanctification* (London, Japan Evangelistic Band, 1931), 2-3.
2. Martin, 478.
3. Guthrie, 638.

NOTES

NOTES

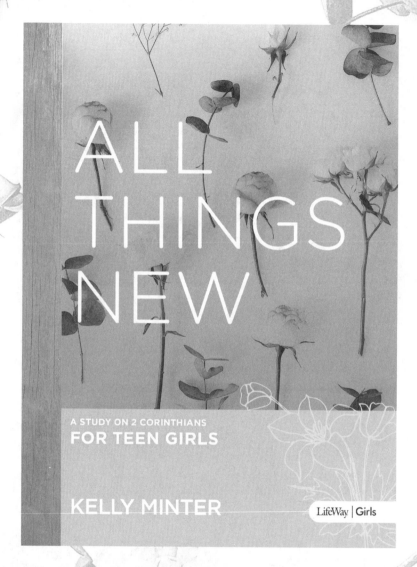

If you loved All Things New, this study is just the beginning.

Dig deeper into the Bible with additional studies from Kelly Minter.

WHAT LOVE IS
The Letters of 1, 2, 3 John
7 sessions

Delve into the Letters of 1, 2, and 3 John, written to encourage followers of Jesus to remain faithful to the truth. Glimpse not only the heart of John but also the heart of Jesus.

Bible Study Book 005635536 $12.99
Leader Kit   005635537 $69.99

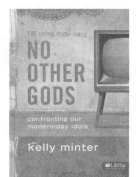

NO OTHER GODS
Confronting Our Modern-Day Idols
8 sessions

Make room for God by dethroning the functional gods that clutter and claim our lives with this first study in The Living Room series.

Bible Study Book 005035500 $12.99

NEHEMIAH
A Heart That Can Break
7 sessions

Nehemiah's heart was so broken for those in need that he left the comfort of his Persian palace to help them. Are you ready to let God break your heart for a hurting, lost world and move you to be the hands and feet of Jesus?

Bible Study Book 005371581 $12.99
Leader Kit   005461775 $69.99

HYMNS & HALLELUJAHS

A melodic album filled with the rich lyrics of beloved hymns alongside new songs from Kelly Minter and other songwriters set to guitar, piano, fiddle, percussion, and other acoustic instruments.

Music CD   005786028 $9.99

RUTH
Loss, Love & Legacy
6 sessions

If you've ever felt devastated, struggled as a stranger in an unfamiliar place, longed to be loved, or wept along the way, you'll find a loyal sister in Ruth. Her journey of unbearable loss, redeeming love, and divine legacy comes alive alongside a companion CD of original songs written and performed by Kelly to engage participants on their spiritual journeys.

Bible Study Book 005189427 $12.99
Music CD   005275025 $12.99

lifeway.com/KellyMinter
800.458.2772 | LifeWay Christian Stores

LifeWay | Women

Pricing and availability subject to change without notice.

BRING KELLY'S

cultivate

TO YOUR CHURCH!

Biblically focused & stylistically simple,
Cultivate Events offer a time to seek God's Word, worship with an acoustic ensemble,
enjoy the warmth of community and prayer, and focus on living missionally.

If your church or women's ministry is interested in hosting a Cultivate event
featuring Kelly Minter, or attending an upcoming event, please email
info@kellyminter.com or visit Kelly's website at
www.kellyminter.com/cultivate

WILL YOU JOIN
Kelly Minter
IN CARING FOR THE POOR, THE ORPHANED & FORGOTTEN?

JUSTICE & MERCY INTERNATIONAL IS A NON-PROFIT, CHRIST-CENTERED ORGANIZATION THAT CARES FOR THE VULNERABLE AND FORGOTTEN IN THE AMAZON AND MOLDOVA.

FIND OUT HOW YOU CAN HELP BY VISITING WWW.JUSTICEANDMERCY.ORG

Justice & mercy INTERNATIONAL